"An opinionated guide to Sin City eateries, [with] a great premise."
—Kitty Bean Yancey, *USA Today*

❧ ❦ ❧

"If you spend much time in Las Vegas, you need this book."
—S. Irene Virbila, *Los Angeles Times*

❧ ❦ ❧

"Expect kitchen knives to be sharpened. The comments—both sweet and sour—are funny, biting, candid, and relevant."
—Robin Leach

❧ ❦ ❧

"A lively and smart guide to the city [from] a Rat Pack of reviewers."
—Julia Moskin, *New York Times*

❧ ❦ ❧

"Indispensable annual guidebook … *Eating Las Vegas* is written with passion and authority."
—Karen Tina Harrison
Luxury Travel Expert, About.com

D0089231

EATING
LAS VEGAS

EATING
LAS VEGAS

THE 50 ESSENTIAL
RESTAURANTS

John Curtas | Greg Thilmont | Mitchell Wilburn

HUNTINGTON PRESS
LAS VEGAS, NEVADA

EATING LAS VEGAS
The 50 Essential Restaurants

Published by
Huntington Press
3665 Procyon Street
Las Vegas, NV 89103
Phone (702) 252-0655
e-mail: books@huntingtonpress.com

Copyright ©2017, John Curtas, Greg Thilmont, Mitchell Wilburn

ISBN: 978-1-935396-73-4
$14.95US

Production & Design: Laurie Cabot
Cover Photo: Bazaar Meat, SLS Las Vegas
Special acknowledgment to Tazeen Shazreh Ahmed who served as the official
photographer for this edition.

Inside Photos: Spoon ©Torsten Schon, Dreamstime.com; MGM Resorts International:
viii, 8, 18, 20, 24, 36, 56, 68, 74, 84, 90, 92, 94, 96, 102, 112, 114, 143, 144, 149, 168, 172,
206, 209, 248; Venetian/Palazzo: xii, 34, 38, 50, 141, 164, 203, 210, 216, 229; Mandarin
Oriental/Bread & Butter Public Relations: 6, 104, 147; SLS Las Vegas: 10, 46, 155, 191;
Douglas Friedman/MGM Resorts: 12; Vox Solid Communications: 14, 60, 138, 166, 232;
Cosmopolitan of Las Vegas: 16, 58, 150; John Curtas: 22, 110, 122, 126, 130, 135, 163,
174, 175, 177, 189, 205, 213; Greg Thilmont: 26, 180; Wynn Las Vegas/Barbara Kraft:
28, 102, 148; Wynn Las Vegas/Robert Miller: 30; Andiron: 32, 140; Peter Harasty: 40,
212; Chada Vegas: 42; Jeff Green: 48, 142; District One: 52; Due Forni: 54; Glutton: 62,
196; Scott Roeben/Caesars Entertainment: 64, 204; The Goodwich/Theo van Soest: 66,
116; Fingerprint Communications: 70, 156, 182, 238; Hiroyoshi Japanese Cuisine: 72;
Kabuto: 76, 179; Bill Huges: 80, 98, 175; Marche Bacchus: 82; Caesars Entertainment:
86, 100, 142, 162, 169; Amanda B. Lee: 88, 188; Yonaka Japanese Restaurant: 108, 178;
Jessica Roe: 120, 227; Messina Heisenberg: 160; Golden Steer Steakhouse: 111; Tazeen
Ahmed: 121, 124, 125, 127, 131, 132, 133, 134, 136, 137, 146, 151, 157, 158, 159, 161,
170, 176, 184, 187, 188, 190, 199, 202; Jasper Ibe: 129; Island Malaysian Cuisine: 135;
Ellis Island 143; Restaurant Guy Savoy, Paris: 146; Gordon Ramsay/Caesars Entertain-
ment: 154, 219; Fat Choy: 153, 185; Nora's Cuisine: 167; Settebello: 171; Sushi Mon:
181; Forte European Tapas: 185; Battista's Hole in the Wall: 191; Four Queens: 192;
Italian American Club: 193; Peppermill Restaurant and Lounge: 194; Le Thai: 198; the
D: 200, 208; Bootlegger: 201; STK: 211; Mint Indian Bistro: 214; CraftHaus: 218; Public
House: 220; Haute Living Vegas: 223, 229; Bunkhouse Saloon: 224; Double Down Saloon: 225; Money Plays: 226; Velveteen Rabbit: 228, 231; Herbs & Rye: 230

Dedications

John Curtas
For my sons Anthony and Alex—the fruit of my loins and the apples of my eye and the best damn dining companions any father ever had.

Greg Thilmont
For my mom, Amelia "Mimi" Thilmont, who would let me order lobster at fancy restaurants every now and then when I was a little kid.

Mitchell Wilburn
To everyone who has bet on me to succeed, given me a chance, or just believed in a short balding nerd who loves eating, drinking, and writing.

BLACK AND BLUE TUNA AT SAGE

Contents

Section I—The Top Ten

Section II—The Rest of the Best

Section III—Additional Recommendations

Section IV—Index and Maps

Contents

xi

CARNE CRUDA AT CARNEVINO

Foreword

by Barbara Fairchild

The first time I ever saw my dad tip a maitre d' for a better table was in Las Vegas. It was in a post-Rat Pack, pre-Steve Wynn time frame, and this little gesture was a revelation: Yes, my dad was a recognizable character actor with a successful career, but still, money was tight, so *tipping* someone to get a better seat? Wow. That's when I knew that this was no ordinary town.

Flash forward to the 1990s. As executive editor of *Bon Appetit* magazine, I was helping to put the finishing touches on "Desert Storm," the first of what would be many stories we would do on the dining scene in Las Vegas. Yes, the nineties: I knew once Wolfgang Puck and Jean-Louis Palladin came to town, there would be no looking back.

It seems that I was right. And so here we are: Or rather, here you are, with this excellent book in your hands, one that is far more than just a mere "guide to local restaurants" or whatever the standard jargon would be. The intrepid trio that put this together—the inimitable John Curtas, and the equally discerning Greg Thilmont and Mitchell Wilburn—have decades of dining-out war stories in Vegas. So they have made sure that *Eating Las Vegas* is *the definitive* book of its kind.

I heartily agree: It's exhaustively researched, excellently written with great wit and style, and includes beautiful photographs to help set the mood, or in today's vernacular: There's a lot of good food porn in here. Add the easy-to-use format and you have a book that is a real keeper. The "Top 10" alone is worth the price of admission, and helps make the point that this is no "hotel only" book. These guys know the territory and go all over town to bring you the best—from the Strip to the strip mall. Plus, I don't know any other trio of writers that would include a chapter on chain restaurants, but these three are up to the challenge. For that I have only one word: *courage*.

If I sound enthusiastic, it's because I am. Statistics time and again show that these days, the main reasons people come to Vegas are for dining and shopping. "Gaming" is still a part of it, of course. But where else can you find the concentration of quality and selection like the restaurants featured in these pages? I've often said that in a week's worth of breakfasts, lunches, and dinners here, you could hit just about every major chef in the U.S. and France, with Asia, Italy, and Spain thrown in for the delicious ride. Let this trio of experts help lead the way.

Just last spring, a speaking engagement brought me to Alizé, the Michelin-starred restaurant at the top of the Palms hotel. I was early and the restaurant was fairly empty. The view is spectacular from Alizé—a unique "set-back" perspective of the city—and it gave me pause: Caught between a vivid sunset and the advent of night, the lights below were just coming on. There were the sparkling hotels of the Strip at one end of Las Vegas Boulevard, the Stratosphere and the almost honky-tonk vibe of Fremont Street at the other; planes were coming and going from McCarran International, rush-hour traffic and the low-slung spread of suburbia ran in almost every direction. But where I was standing—silence. No ordinary town. No ordinary book. Extraordinary, indeed.

Introduction

by John Curtas

If you're reading these words, you can congratulate yourself on having the good taste and common sense to buy this book. It means you're passionate about food and restaurants and that you have (or will have) a connection to one of the greatest restaurant cities in the world. It also means you want to dive deeper into food, tasting it more intensely and thinking more thoughtfully about where and what you eat.

Buying this book also means you're a bit old-fashioned. Guidebooks are so 1997, aren't they? In this age of social media and Yelp and Trip Advisor, who needs an actual curated, thoroughly researched, printed, and bound dining guide, in hand, to decide where to go out to eat? Well, avid eaters like myself, for one, and I'm guessing that by buying this book, you and I are on the same page.

The need for restaurant guidebooks occurred to me many times over the past year, as I traveled around the U.S., Europe, and Asia, looking for the best places to eat. Like many a wayfaring gourmand, I enjoy planning a trip almost as much as going on one. Back in the day, guidebooks aplenty could tell you where to eat in New York or Paris or Rome. These days, you can't find a pure restaurant guide to any of them. You're left with the blizzard of information on the Internet, a double-edged sword if ever there was one. Sure, Top 10 lists and crowd-sourced opinions are everywhere, but lacking is the voice of food writers who know what they're talking about and want to share their knowledge with you—the better to help you make informed decisions on where to spend your precious dining-out dollars.

And let's face it, as much as the Millennial generation might not agree, thumbing through a ready reference guide is a lot more fun and convenient than staring at your smartphone.

Informed opinion is what this book is all about. It's 200-plus pages of restaurants—both large and small, of great reputation or none at all—that have been visited time and again by the authors. I not-so-humbly claim that no one in the history of Las Vegas has ever, or will ever, eat in more of its restaurants than I have. Since 1981, I've scoured this city in search of the best meal I could find. Greg Thilmont and Mitchell Wilburn have a lot of catching up to do, but in them I've found two able lieutenants who are as hungry for the good stuff as I am.

This is my second edition with these co-authors and the fifth overall. Las Vegas is too important a restaurant city, and too huge a tourist destination, *not* to have its own guidebook. Forty-three million annual visitors have to eat. The population of greater Las Vegas is well over two million hungry souls and rising. We have some of the greatest restaurants in the world, more accomplished chefs than I can count, and an ability to feed every local and tourist the most wonderful food on the planet. From our burgeoning Japanese scene (Yui, Hiroyoshi, Japaneiro, Yuzu, Fish N Bowl, Yonaka, et al.) and new infusions of L.A. Chinese cool (Chengdu Taste) to a resuscitation of some old friends (hello Bouchon, Andiron and Charlie Palmer Steak!), things have gotten even tastier in the past year. Throw in some downtown Vietnam (Le Pho) here and a Mediterranean marvel (Khoury's) there, and you have a town that is as much about its food as it is about gambling, nightclubs, shopping, and conventions. The party-as-a-verb crowd has nothing on intrepid gastronauts and destination-dining denizens when it comes to keeping this city humming.

As with the last edition, we break this book down into the Top 10 (listed alphabetically), and then the Rest of the Best, 40 more stellar restaurants also listed alphabetically. In the second half of the book, you'll find scores of hidden gems and worthy contenders. Chinatown gets its own section, as do steakhouses, because our town excels in these two areas of eating like almost none other in America (plus, in this edition we've added a mini-stand-alone section featuring Las Vegas' outstanding French cuisine).

The 50 Essential Restaurants define our dining culture right now, the places that are putting out the best food Las Vegas has to offer, where I'd take a visiting food writer, critic, or imperious gastronome if they asked me to personally guide them on a month-long tour of "eating Las Vegas." I've guided people, literally and figuratively, through the restaurants of Las Vegas for 21 years now. Because eating Las Vegas is what I do, and what Greg Thilmont and Mitchell Wilburn do, better than anyone. It's also, dear reader, what you're soon to be doing, more knowledgeably and enjoyably than ever.

Price Designations

At the top of each review is one of four price designations: $25 or less, $25-$75, $75-$125, or $125 and up. They provide a general guide to what it will cost you to dine there, based on the per-person price of an appetizer, an entrée, a side or dessert, and one or two lower-priced cocktails.

Who's In / Who's Out

After the publication of last-year's edition, we were asked many times what changes had been made in the lists. So we don't have to answer that question a couple of hundred times again this year, here's a quick-and-dirty culinary box score.

In

Top Ten—Carbone, Sage, Yui Edomae Sushi
Essential 50—Andiron, B&B Ristorante, Bouchon, Chengdu Taste, Due Forni Pizza & Wine, Harvest by Roy Ellamar, Hiroyoshi, Khoury's, MR CHOW, rm Seafood, Stripsteak

Out

Top Ten (but still in the 50)—Guy Savoy, Joël Robuchon, Twist by Pierre Gagnaire
Essential 50—Andre's (closed), Artisanal (closed), El Dorado Cantina, Inyo Asian Restaurant (closed), Japanese Cuisine by Omae (closed), Lulu's Bread & Breakfast, Mizumi, Monta Ramen, Rose. Rabbit. Lie., Yardbird, Yusho

TWIST AT MANDARIN ORIENTAL

Section I

The Top Ten

BARDOT BRASSERIE (STRIP)

French

Aria at CityCenter
(877) 230-2742
aria.com
Mon.-Fri., 5:30-11 p.m.; Sat. & Sun., 9:30 a.m.-11 p.m.
$75-$125

CURTAS

When Michael Mina announced he was closing American Fish at Aria and replacing it with a classic French brasserie, more than a few foodies scoffed. Didn't he know that this is the age of tiny tables, minuscule plates, insulting noise levels, and uncomfortable everything? Hadn't someone told him that traditional French style is about as hip as a dickey? And that Croque Madame and salad Niçoise were old hat by the Clinton era?

They might have told him, but we're happy he didn't listen. Instead, what he did was bring forth a drop-dead-delicious ode to the golden era of brass, glass, and béchamel-drenched sandwiches— hearty platters of wine-friendly food that many think went out of style with tasseled menus, but didn't. It just took a break for a decade.

With BB, the reasons all of these recipes became famous to begin with has come roaring back, to the delight of diners who want to be coddled and cosseted with cuisine, not challenged and annoyed.

Mina had the prescience to know this, and the good sense to hire Executive Chef Josh Smith to execute his vision. Smith is an American through and through, but obviously has a deep feeling for this food, and every night (and via the best weekend brunch in town), he proves why classics never go out of style and overwrought, overthought, multi-course tasting menus may soon go the way of the supercilious sommelier.

Make no mistake, Bardot Brasserie is a throwback restaurant, but a throwback that captures the heart and soul of real French food like none of its competition. It harkens to an age of comfort food from a country that pretty much invented the term. What sets it apart is the attention to detail. Classics like steak frites and quiche are clichés to be sure, but here they're done with such aplomb, you'll feel like you're on the Left Bank of Paris, only with better beef. The pâté de campagne (country house-made pâté) is a wondrous evocation of pressed pork of the richest kind, and the escargots in puff pastry show how a modern chef can update a classic without sacrificing the soul of the original recipe. The skate wing suffers not at all from being 6,000 miles from the Champs Elysée, and the lobster Thermidor—bathed in Béarnaise and brandy cream—is a glorious testament to the cuisine of Escoffier.

Most of all, though, Bardot Brasserie is an homage to the great homey restaurants of France. By going old school, Michael Mina has set a new standard in Franco-American style and made us realize what we were missing all along.

GET THIS: Lobster Thermidor; skate wing; Croque Madame; onion soup grantinee; foie gras parfait; steak tartare; duck wings à l'Orange; king crab crêpe; seared foie gras Lyonnaise; frisee aux lardons; sole meuniere; chicken roti; oak-smoked Duroc pork chop; brunch.

WILBURN

Where so many have failed to "bring back the classics" in a half-hearted culinary dry-hump, Bardot Basserie is literally a time portal into the days of Escoffier. It's meticulous, obsessive, perfectionist French cuisine in just about the most beautiful room on the Strip.

BAZAAR MEAT BY JOSE ANDRES [STRIP] | Steakhouse

SLS Las Vegas
(702) 761-7610
slslasvegas.com
Sun.-Thurs., 5:30-10 p.m.; Fri. & Sat., 5:30-10:30 p.m.
$75-$125

THILMONT

Do you dream of cotton-candy-spun foie gras? I know I do, after experiencing it at Bazaar Meat by José Andrés at SLS.

Skewered tidbits of unctuous goose liver are lightly dusted with nutty amaranth flour. Then they're playfully cocooned in circus-style house-made spun sugar. They're a theater of cuisine on the tongue—cotton candy implodes, foie gras melts, and amaranth grit kicks in for a hint of tangible substance in an otherwise nearly ethereal gustatory happening. It matches perfectly with the house "smoked" Manhattan cocktail, by the way.

This is just the most popular appetizer the haute-culinary butcher-as-showman José Andrés has created at his cathedral of meats. In a movie-like scene of smoky cooking stations and vivid arrays of prepared sliced viands, Chef Andrés oversees a sorcerer's studio of blazing cuisine. Sitting in Bazaar Meat, which has a smart-but-comfortable décor by the famed Philippe Starck, is never passive. It's an interactive-style joint of many (animal) parts.

Dinners at Bazaar Meat are perfectly started with a wide array of charcuterie—some imported, like pricey Jamón Ibérico de Bellota, the porcine gift of black-footed pigs that feed on acorns near Salamanca, or fine domestic viands like wild-boar sausage from Creminelli in Salt Lake City. Also, Andrés' tartares are finely diced, such as sirloin with Colman's Savora mustard, egg yolk, HP Sauce, and anchovy. For a twist away from toast points, soft Parker House rolls are served on the side in a cast-iron cradle.

Though this all sounds very terrestrial, Bazaar Meat has an advanced raw bar, where you can order chilled slices of live scallops or goeduck and shells of oysters either fresh or grilled. A number of caviar flights are available at incrementally increasing prices; starting at rainbow trout and ending up at Petrossian sturgeon is how this roe road goes.

Of course, this place is turf-forward in the end. The list of chops is extensive, including planks of Holstein rib steak, classic Chateaubriand, pork loin from Quebec, New Zealand lamb, and so on. And if you want to smash your piggy bank, gather a group and order the whole Spanish suckling pig. It's a culinary extravaganza all its own.

Oh yes, gazpacho, cooked vegetables, and salads are on the menu, too, in this otherwise protein-centric *palacio*.

GET THIS: Cotton-candy foie gras; gazpacho shots; steak tartare; "smoke-and-ice" oysters; beef and Parmesan grissini; chef's selection of cured meats; Washugyu/Angus flat-iron steak; suckling pig; the Foieffle; croquetas de Jamón; Ferran Adria olives; whole roasted turbot; Beefsteak tomato tartare; Vaca Vieja (old beef) ribeye tasting; tortilla sacromonte (sweetbread/kidney omelet); Butifarra spiral sausage.

CURTAS

Calling it a meat emporium is a bit unfair, since the seafood and wacky Spanish creations are every bit as good as the steaks. I'll put Bazaar Meat (and Carnevino) up against any steakhouse in the country, any day.

Aria at CityCenter
(877) 230-2742
aria.com
5:30-11 p.m., daily
$75-$125

CURTAS

Alan Richman, in reviewing the original Carbone in New York City three years ago, pointed out that all Italian-American restaurants are past their prime. He compared them with Al Pacino at the end of *Godfather III*: desiccated, dissipated, and haunted by the memories of better days. Mario Carbone and Rich Torrisi are trying to single-handedly buck this trend and resuscitate the genre by presenting an upscale, very expensive, and theatrical Italian-American joint with excellent Eye-talian food in large portions at jaw-dropping prices. If the hordes packing this place every night are any indication, by and large they're succeeding.

Carbone Las Vegas opened late last year with its New York pedigree intact and from the get-go, a reservation has been almost impossible to get. That reputation draws them in by making everyone feel as if they're in an old-school movie while they're eating there. The groovy '60s' sound track plays just the right mix of crooners and doo-wop and the atmosphere, from the tuxedoed waiters to the flaming tableside preparations, is a throwback in all the best ways. Our suggestion is to go with a crowd, go light on the booze, and be ready to do a lot of family-style noshing. That way you'll spread the cost around and try lots of dishes that would overwhelm a two-top.

Like what? Like duck-fat fried potatoes Louie, so rich they should have their own tax bracket, or very spicy rigatoni in vodka sauce that's easily enough for four to share. The $50 veal parmigiana caused quite a stir when it debuted back in the Big Apple in 2012; in Las Vegas, they charge $64 without so much as a tube of K-Y on the side. No one is batting an eye these days, so who am I to argue? Nowhere is Vegas' status as the most expensive dining city in America confirmed more than by looking at Carbone's prices.

As for wine, it's a very good Italian list, one of the best in the city, though it's best approached with your accountant in tow and a second mortgage. On the plus side, the sommeliers are super nice and very good looking.

Like the prices, everything about Carbone is over the top. Which makes it perfect for Vegas, and perfect for our Top 10.

GET THIS: Meatballs (not on the menu, you have to ask); minestrone soup; all pastas (especially rigatoni in vodka sauce); veal parmigiana; pork chop with peppers; flaming bananas.

WILBURN

The only restaurant in this category of super-precise classic Euro-country food besides Bardot. Carbone differs from its French neighbor in the décor (Carbone's is fancier) and the prices (Carbone's are higher), but other than that, what Bardot is to Croque Madame and lobster Thermidor, Carbone is to veal parm and whole branzino.

CARNEVINO (STRIP)

Steakhouse

Palazzo
(702) 789-4141
carnevino.com
5-11 p.m., daily;
Taverna: noon-midnight
$75-$125

CURTAS

Carnevino isn't just one of the best steakhouses in Las Vegas; it might be the best steakhouse in the country. It's also, on any given night, one of the best Italian restaurants in America. Throw in a killer cocktail program, a spacious and inviting lounge, a world-class wine list, plus a little dynamo named Nicole Brisson—who makes the whole thing run like a fine-tuned watch—and you have a one-of-a-kind only-in-Vegas experience that deserves to be a lot more famous than it is. If Brisson were doing this kind of work in New York or Los Angeles, she would've graced numerous magazines and television shows by now.

As it is, Carnevino exists in a world of its own, a sui generis blend of superior Italian food and the country's best beef. Its "riserva" steaks are justifiably famous and you have to call ahead to reserve one that's been aged anywhere from 60 to 150 days—what Brisson considers the "sweet spot." Do so and you'll taste beef like you've never encountered it before. They're not for everyone (and the regular dry-aged ribeye and strip are otherworldly in their own right), but if you have the coin and the palate, you'll pay for the privilege of eating the most unique gamey steaks in the world.

If beef ain't your bag, take heart. The pastas, antipasti, and fish will more than satisfy your craving for a taste of Italia. Thus does this kitchen also dazzle with everything from house-cured salumi, such as coppa, lardo, and lonza, to a variety of pastas as diverse as corn agnolotti, lobster agnolini, and linguine with crab, jalapeños, and cipollini. Put these together with an abundance of locally sourced products and you have that rarest of creatures: a huge celebrity-chef-driven Las Vegas restaurant that's also very much a part of the local food community.

GET THIS: Riserva steaks; dry-aged bone-in ribeye; New York strip; lamb chops "Scottadita"; all house-cured salumi; carne crudo alla Piedmontese (steak tartare); house-cured pastrami; grilled octopus; shrimp alla diavolo; linguine with crab and jalapeños; bucatina all'amatriciana; ricotta and egg ravioli; grilled sweetbreads; veal chop; osso buco alla milanese; all pastas.

WILBURN

The country for steak is the United States of America, and in the U.S. of A., the city for steak is Las Vegas, and in Las Vegas, the pinnacle of steakhouses is—with little argument—Carnevino, in every way conceivable. End of discussion.

Cosmopolitan
(702) 698-7000
ebyjoseandres.com
Tues.-Sun., 5:30 & 8:30 p.m. seatings
$125 and up

CURTAS

My affection and respect for é by José Andrés are inversely pro-portional to my dislike of molecular food. But five years into its very successful run at the Cosmopolitan—as a restaurant within a restau-rant (Jaleo)—I finally showed up and allowed his chefs to wear me down with a passion and precision you usually don't find in Las Ve-gas restaurants, through a panoply of micro'd this and tweezed that, served to a mere 16 diners a night.

Once you score a reservation (done online and not as hard as it sounds, although it may take a week or two to bag a couple of seats), walk into the sanctum sanctorum and hang on tight. What you're in for are 25+ courses of the most dazzling cooking you're likely to find anywhere in America. It's a hoot of an experience, a must for any ardent foodie. It's definitely not for traditionalists, or someone who demands large proteins with his evening meal, or those who like a few carbs with their foamy this and immersion-circulated that. (There are practically none.)

What you'll also get, if you're lucky, are the sweetest clams you'll ever taste under espuma (foam), molecular olives that are still a treat (no matter how many times you've had them), and an Ibérico ham soup that is as odd and intense a broth as you'll ever experience. Man does not live by molecule manipulation alone, so expect gorgeous fish and meat courses to round out your meal and meld perfectly with the (mostly Spanish) wines chosen for the occasion.

From what we observed, the average customer for this experience is an upper-middle-class Gen-X gastronaut, for whom this sort of experience is a necessary station on the cross of their gourmet education. Aging Boomers may consider all this molecular folderol to be the equivalent of kids playing in a gastronomic sandbox, but take heart: You will still be blown away by five chefs employing every trick in the book to satisfy and sate your culinary curiosity.

GET THIS: There is no ordering, so whatever they're making is what you'll get. With any luck, you'll be served José's sangria; beet gazpacho; José's tacos; oyster and oyster; Ibérico ham soup; clams in orange espuma; Spanish pizza; morels en papillote; fluke with caviar; crema Catalana egg; ribeye beef cap; plus a dozen other eye-popping creations.

THILMONT

Months after entering the inner sanctum of gustatory magic that is é by José Andrés, I can't stop raving about my long evening there. Frankly, it's one of the most extraordinary dining tableaus I've ever experienced. Consider the representative ideas of a translucent globe filled with cava that explodes in your mouth like effervescent fireworks or a morsel of steamed skate that looks like delicate porcelain sculpture. Sure, there's plenty of liquid-nitrogen fog and edible trompe-l'œil happening in this demonstration dining extravaganza, but it's friendly, informative, de void of pretense, and totally full of cool factor. And here are a couple of hints: When the steak course comes around, get that ribeye bone for gnawing! Drink plenty of sherry, too.

L'ATELIER DE JOEL ROBUCHON (STRIP)   French

MGM Grand
(702) 891-7358
mgmgrand.com
5-10:30 p.m., daily
$125 and up

CURTAS

The only thing to dislike about L'Atelier is its infuriatingly inconvenient location. Unless you're staying in the MGM, to get to it, you
must first endure the worst parking garage on the Strip or confront
the slowest valet service in the universe, run the gauntlet of half-
drunk and poorly dressed tourists (or is it the other way around?),
then traverse the length of one of the world's largest and most
confusing casinos. These annoyances pile up quickly when you're
hungry and by the time you actually get to the far reaches of this
behemoth of a building, you can be excused for being in a very bad
mood. The good news is all will be forgiven as soon as you take your
first bite.

Before you get to that, however, the menu can be a bit daunting.
There are small bites here and prix-fixes there, and seasonal menus
and degustation suggestions, and entrées and appetizers that don't
fall in either category. There's even a killer vegetarian menu for those
who are so inclined. So, instead of being intimidated or confused, do

what I do: Close your eyes and point. No matter what shows up, be it flaky cod with eggplant in a dashi broth, the best lobster salad in the universe, a hanger steak from heaven, or a buttery spaghetti topped with soft-boiled egg, sea urchin, and caviar, you can be assured of a drop-dead-delicious forkful.

L'Atelier, like its big brother Joël Robuchon next door, has been open for 10 years now and under the watchful eye of Executive Chef Steve Benjamin, it hasn't skipped a beat. In many ways, it's better than ever. So good, in fact, we can almost forgive its inaccessibility. On second thought, if it was easier to get to, I'd be here every week.

GET THIS: La Morue; flaky cod with eggplant in dashi broth; Le Burger; Ris de Veau (sweetbreads); grilled seasonal vegetables; Les Spaghettis (spaghetti with soft egg, urchin, and caviar); L'Onglet (hanger steak with pommes frites); Le Caille (free-range quail stuffed with foie gras); Le Kampachi (soy-glazed kampachi with endive salad); Le Homard (lobster salad with sherry vinaigrette); Le Jambon (Ibérico de Bellota: Spanish ham with toasted tomato bread); anything and everything for dessert.

THILMONT

L'Atelier de Joël Robuchon is an impeccable dining experience. The prix-fixe dinners are, indeed, the way to go here. In fact, deciding which selection of diverse plates to experience is one of the charms of the establishment. Also, it's the perfect place in Vegas for the solo epicure.

WILBURN

The funner funkier little brother of the bigger Robuchon next door, the food here is definitely worthy of a Top Ten spot. These kinds of deconstructions and imaginative combinations made Robuchon famous, but Chef Steve Benjamin putting his spin on things is what really sets this apart from your usual Michelin-starred semi-fine haute French.

The Top Ten

Bellagio
(702) 693-8100
bellagio.com
Tues.-Sun., 5-10 p.m.
$75-$125

WILBURN

The characteristic of Las Vegas "transplant" restaurants, too often sub-standard clones of their successful brothers, is something with which the detached elite of food writing will critique this city. They'll call it a cash grab, a Disneyland version, anything to strip the specter of "authenticity" from a place that pressed $1 buffets and $5 steaks on the American zeitgeist. There might be examples where they would be right, but with Le Cirque in Bellagio, they're dead-ass wrong.

When Steve Wynn invested every last shred of his sanity and taste into what is undoubtedly the crown jewel of his legacy, the notorious haute cuisine and impeccable marksman-like service that made Le Cirque a Manhattan legend seemed a bridge too far. Every detail, every stitch, and every button were labored over, not only by Wynn, but by the Maccioni family members themselves. Patriarch Sirio Maccioni, the man who transformed American fine dining in the 1970s, put his oldest son, Mario, in the captain's chair, a position he helmed with the assistance of General Manager Supreme Ivo Angelov, for a decade. The menu still honors their legendary Le Cirque classics, like the Blanquette de Lapin (rabbit symphony) with Riesling cream and spätzel.

The Le Cirque concept, the one that garnered fame for turning executive chefs out into the world (like Daniel Boulud), still shines with the current Exec, culinary wünderkind Wilfried Bergerhausen. Give a talented chef an elite staff, a sterling-clad standard, and a laughably large food-cost budget, and he'll deliver greatness. In the most accessible opulence Vegas has to offer, Chef Wil sends out a menu that sparkles: some Le Cirque classics, along with many fresh, dazzling, mind-bogglingly inspired dishes. The various tasting menus range from the decadent (and very "Vegas") La Caille—quail farci stuffed with foie gras and black truffle, perched in a potato mousseline "tree" with black truffle "leaves"—to the eye-catching experiment of Maryland blue crab, avocado, and a veritable tectonic plate of oscietra caviar.

GET THIS: Everything. Blanquette de lapin; le crabe et caviar Osetra; la caille; le risotto du marché; petit boule de chocolate; Maryland blue crab and Russian caviar "ocean water smoke"; sautéed foie gras; potato-crusted sea bass; Colorado lamb with baby turnips; Japanese A-5 sirloin with oxtail and Bordelaise sauce; crème brûlée; vegetarian tasting menu, or preferably, the largest tasting menu you can afford, with whatever wine Super-Somme Frédéric Montandon is excited about.

CURTAS

Adam Tihany's colorful circus tent has held up remarkably well for 17 years and still boasts the most flattering lighting you'll ever eat by. All of it creates a glow of good feeling that starts from the moment you enter and is reinforced by the best service staff in the business. Whether you've been here a dozen times or once, they treat you like a big shot and make everyone from fussy gastronomes to newlyweds feel very special.

RAKU & SWEETS RAKU (WEST)　　　Japanese

see map 1, page 250
5030 Spring Mtn. Road Suites 2 & 3
(702) 367-3511 / (702) 290-7181
raku-grill.com
Raku: Mon.-Sat., 6 p.m.-2 a.m. / Sweets Raku: Thurs.-Tue., 6 p.m.-
midnight; Sat., noon-midnight; Sun., noon-9 p.m.
$25-$75

CURTAS

Raku and Sweets Raku aren't simply places to eat; they're statements of quality and passion, a dedication to excellence that can
no longer be faked or phoned in, either on or off the Strip. You can
thank Japanese émigré Mitsuo Endo for this taste revolution (not
some absentee celebrity chef who treats Vegas like an easy-access
ATM machine). The next great meal you have off the Strip, be it a
humble noodle joint or a fancy chef-driven room, owes more than
a little nod to Endo-san's continuing quest for perfection. It was
he who made Spring Mountain Road a foodie destination, lifting it
above its roots as a forlorn stretch of bargain-basement Asian eats.

Japanese izakaya, oden, and robata cooking was virtually un-
heard of when Raku opened in early 2008. With only his authentic
sensibilities to guide him, Endo has taught Las Vegas just how great
Japanese cooking can be. Izakayas are everywhere these days, strut-
ting their stuff and educating palates like nobody's business, but
Raku, hidden in a corner of a small Spring Mountain Road strip mall,

gave Las Vegas its first taste of binchotan charcoal cooking and pork cheek, beef silver skin, and tomato with bacon and asparagus, which are just as stunning today as they were when the place opened. The agedashi tofu and foie gras egg custard are studies in steamed minimalism, and what this tiny kitchen does with oily fish is legendary. There's a fixed menu of all of the above, but true Japronauts wait for the daily-specials chalk board to come around, then just point and enjoy the ride.

Raku is for a certain type of adventuresome food lover, but its sweet sister parked a few doors down serves finely crafted desserts (and small savory bites, and lunch on weekends) that can either be analyzed, admired for their art, or consumed wholesale, depending on your mood. French technique blended with Japanese precision is a match made in heaven and Sweets Raku takes a back seat to no one when it comes to eye-popping sugar creations.

Endo-san may not be aware of the revolution he started, but I am. *Domo arigato* and *gochisousama* ("Thank you for feeding us"), Mitsuo Endo.

GET THIS RAKU: Agedashi tofu; Kobe beef liver sashimi; ayu nanbantsuke (sweet marinated smelt); beef silver skin ebishinjo (shrimp) souffle; kurobuta pork cheek; fried ice fish; sashimi salad; Raku tofu; poached egg with sea urchin and salmon roe; sunomono salad; Tsukune-grilled ground chicken; Kobe beef liver.

SWEETS RAKU: Seasonal dessert set; les fromages japonaise; foie gras.

THILMONT

These two rooms are so distinct in visual décor, it's striking. But they're united by inventiveness and quality in taste. At it's core, Izakaya is a pretty rough-and-tumble sake-swillin' cuisine born in bars. But it's elevated at the original Raku. Over at Sweets, the confections are like jeweled works of art. Stunning all around.

SAGE (STRIP)   Contemporary

Aria at CityCenter
(877) 230-2742
aria.com
Mon.-Sat., 6-10:30 p.m.
$75-$125

WILBURN

If you had to put real money on one restaurant in the Aria to truly be Michelin-worthy, every bet would be on Sage. It's one of the few outposts of Shawn McClain outside his home city of Chicago and it has nearly every hallmark of a spot vying to pry a few of those coveted orange asterisks from their covetous French hands. If the pokers those tire-company employees keep in their rectums are ever removed, I'd go as far as saying that awarding Sage only one star would be a snub.

For the chefs running it, it's half-playground, half-proving ground. Aside from a little bit of veto power flexed by Shawn, it's definitely a collaborative effort by the clogs on the ground. The longstanding man in charge of running Sage and sister restaurants Five50 and Libertine Social, Richard Caramota, and the group of sous are voices carefully heard in the kitchen, but the Chef de Cuisine is, to borrow a metaphor, the quarterback of this team.

Chef Chris Hessinger has been all over the world, working in the most prestigious spots and picking up a menagerie of unique techniques. Some dishes, like his Kaluga caviar starter, start with the classic accoutrements of shallot and crème fraîche, using a hearty quenelle of the eggs themselves, and dab them on a finger sandwich of one entire sous vide egg yolk. The yolk is poached in a very small temperature window that turns it into a translucent, malleable, infinitely creamy dollop. The big celebrity of Sage is the foie gras crème brûlée, a permanent menu item that people come in specifically to enjoy. I've had around 200 different foie dishes in my lifetime and this still ranks among the most memorable—and dare I say life-changing? There's even a veal-cheek dish that builds off a potent Hungarian goulash (a "paprika jus" on the menu), adding pickled maitake mushrooms and onions and a bed of herbed spaetzle. Desserts follow suit in this same spirit, wines and cocktails as well.

The only thing Sage is meek about is the dining-room music, a kind of non-specific background-blending techno.

The entire menu, especially the chef's tasting menu, is full of dishes that are brave enough to explode with flavors where most chefs wouldn't dare; that truly is the charm of Sage.

GET THIS: Foie gras crème brûlée; veal sweetbreads; Kaluga caviar; veal cheeks; heirloom roasted carrot; grilled Spanish octopus; spring lamb; Iberico "Secreto" pork; a fine glass of absinthe at the end of the meal.

CURTAS

High ceilings and dramatic décor set the stage for some of Las Vegas' most dramatic food. I agree with young Wilburn that everything about this place is Michelin-worthy, and if it were located in almost any other city in America, the national food press would constantly shower it with major awards. As it is, the public and press tend to take it for granted. But serious gastronomes do not. The seven-course tasting menu is a flat-out steal at $150, but you won't want to miss the standards on the menu—foie gras brûlée, roasted sweetbreads, Kushi oysters with piquillo peppers—either. The other conundrum you'll have is deciding when to pry yourself from the long and elegant bar, where the whiskeys, absinthe, and cocktails will keep you transfixed far past the dinner hour.

YUI EDOMAE SUSHI (WEST)

Japanese

see map 1, page 250
3460 Arville Street Suite HS
(702) 202-2408
yuisushi.com
Mon.-Sat., 6-10:30 p.m.
$75-$125

CURTAS

Yui is obscure in location and impossible to see from the street – both of which lend just the right amount of Edomae (Tokyo-style) mystery to your experience. Don't be intimidated, though. If you're open to eating sushi the real way, which is to say the Japanese way, you will have the greatest raw-fish-eating experience in Las Vegas, and probably the best Wagyu beef-eating one as well.

Once you secure a reservation (definitely call ahead), you'll be greeted by the gracious and beautiful Tomoko-san, who will lead you past a sliding screen door into the land of serene sushi and sashimi so good, you'll think you're tasting these pristine fish for the first time. Just as terrific is the true, birth-certified, Japanese A-5 Wagyu, delicately grilled over white smokeless charcoal. No one puts a finer point on these things than the Land of the Rising Sun, and the nuances of flavor and texture can sometimes be subtle to the point of invisibility. But like all things exquisite, if you take the time to learn about them, you will be richly rewarded.

Where you'll reap these rewards will either be at the eight-seat sushi bar or one of the three booths facing the chefs (led by chef/owner Gen Mizoguchi, the sushi master who put Kabuto on the map) as they work. Only two menus are offered: a nigiri tasting consisting of five courses (including 10 individual pieces of sushi) for $68, and an omakase ("chef's choice") menu for $120. The latter gets you those same 10 pieces of careful selected and sliced sushi (all of it sitting atop slightly warmed and carefully vinegared rice of almost unbelievable delicacy), along with appetizer, soup, sashimi, and grilled items. What shows up will be food of such beautiful simplicity that you may have to pinch yourself to remember that you're in Las Vegas. The rice is so perfect, you can count the grains in your mouth as you're eating it, and the fish—everything from baby sea bass to kamashita (collar) fatty tuna—is a revelation, and an education, in seafood. This is purist sushi for people who enjoy parsing the differences in texture between cuts of yellowtail, or those who go gaga over ikura (salmon roe) and kawahagi (leather blow fish).

The Japanese credo seems to be: Get out of the way and let the ingredient speak for itself. Seasonings and heat are always applied with a minimalist's touch, and whatever accents there are should, literally, barely touch the food. Thus do these chefs dedicate their lives to crafting each bite into something exquisite, a piece of food that creates a bond between the animal, the chef, and the customer. It's a bond that all chefs hope to achieve, but that Japanese chefs have turned into an art form. "Yui" roughly translates into that "unity between the chef and his diners," according to Gen-san. Put yourself in his hands and you'll feel the connection for yourself.

GET THIS: Nigiri sushi; omakase menu; Wagyu beef.

WILBURN

If Kabuto was Gen-san's dissertation on Edomae-style sushi, Yui is his master's thesis. If your obsession with rare and secretive fish cuts is as deep as your pockets, this will be as close as you can get to sushi perfection in Sin City. Yui Edomae has truly proven itself to be a world-class sushi destination, worthy of a Top Ten spot in Vegas or any city in America.

PEAKY TOE CRAB SALAD AT WYNN LAS VEGAS

Section II

The Rest of the Best

ALLEGRO (STRIP)
Italian

Wynn Las Vegas
(702) 770-2040
wynnlasvegas.com
Mon.-Fri., 3 p.m.-6 a.m.; Sat.-Sun., 10 a.m.-6 a.m.
$25-$75

CURTAS

Since taking over the restaurant formerly known as Stratta (and as Corsa Cucina before that) three years ago, Executive Chef Enzo Febbraro has made this place sing in ways it hasn't sung since Steven Kalt left the premises in 2007. Febbraro is a Neapolitan by birth and a basso profundo by cooking temperament. Whether he's pounding a veal chop into pizza-sized impressiveness or rolling and roasting monkfish in house-made pancetta, you'll know from the first bite you're in the hands of a master. Deep flavors are the rule here, plus a palpable sense of how to intermingle proteins with produce and build on the tastes of both with a judicious use of accents and herbs. Does anyone in town make a better Marsala? Or osso buco? Emphatically no. Neither can many Italians compete with his carpaccio or clams casino. The Food Gal (my significant other) goes crazy for his pizzas (truth be told, they're the best pies of any full-service restaurant in Vegas), and yours truly (a noted beet hater) has even been seen polishing off a plate of Febbraro's beet, bean, and pear salad.

If seafood's your thing, don't miss the Calamarata, a winy stew of monkfish and lobster, or the Risotto Pescatora, which will knock you over with its intensity.

And we haven't even mentioned the pastas yet, the best things on the menu. If you're the sort who likes a rosemary-pepper bite with your scialatielli (and let's face it, who doesn't?), then the carbonara-tossed pasta will make you want to swim in its eggy delights. Ditto the meaty layered baked lasagna that somehow manages the feat of being hearty, rib-sticking, and delicate all at the same time.

The desserts and breads are top-notch, as is almost everything that comes out of the Wynn/Encore's bakeshop, and the wine list is well-matched to the food and not quite as bend-you-over-and-hand-the-Vaseline-oriented as some wine cards at the tonier Wynn-core joints. Another plus: They stay open late, really late, 6 a.m. every morning, making this a mecca for club goers, inveterate gamblers, and the soon-to-be hung over.

GET THIS: All pastas; pizza margherita; beet and frisée salad; clams casino; carpaccio; mozzarella platter; prosciutto platter; veal Marsala; lamb osso buco; veal chop parmigiana; risotto pescatora; basically everything on the friggin' menu.

THILMONT

Mamma mia! *Italiana fantastica* is happening at Allegro in the Wynn. A native Neapolitan, Chef Enzo Febbraro's kitchen creates selections like eggplant parmigiana, house-made meatballs, potato gnocchi Bolognese, and veal Marsala that are savory and satisfying in a bustling friendly room. The seafood risotto and osso buco are absolute standouts. There are numerous vegetarian, and even vegan, offerings, to boot, along with fine pizzas, naturally.

ANDIRON STEAK & SEA (WEST)   American

see map 2, page 251
1720 Festival Plaza Drive
(702) 685-8002
andironsteak.com
Mon.-Fri., 11:30 a.m.-2:30 p.m.; Sun., 10 a.m.-2 p.m.;
Mon.-Sat., 5-11 p.m.; Sun., 5-10 p.m.
$75-$125

CURTAS

Downtown Summerlin, a sprawling outdoor mall that is neither down, nor a town, nor downtown of anything, boasts dozens of eateries, most of which aspire to Old Navy levels of cooking quality. Andiron is by far the classiest of these acts and our best off-Strip steakhouse to boot. Its sleek white-on-white décor will put you in mind of the Hamptons and the comfy tables (and first-class bar) set the stage for some serious eating and people-watching.

They get good oysters here and carve and cure sashimi-grade sea-food, but we prefer the crab cake and straight-from-New England lobster roll when diving into the "sea" portion of this menu. Before you get to the bigger proteins, though, be sure to spend some time with the left side of the card, where you'll find beautifully battered artichokes, a terrific steak tartare, and bacon-wrapped matzo balls that are belly bombs in all the best ways. Soups and salads are also strong, along with whatever farm-to-table composition they're whipping up that day. Asparagus with pea shoots, grilled sweet potatoes, and corn soup festooned with lump crab will invariably elicit oohs and aahs from your table. Steaks are cooked over an apricot-wood-burning grill and are priced about $10 less than you'll find 15 miles to the east. They know their cuts (the rib cap, flat iron, and Cowboy ribeye are superb) and they know their char, and management knows how to keep the well-heeled folks and high-maintenance women of Summerlin happy.

About the only thing to balk at is, you guessed it, the wine list. It has a number of interesting bottles, all priced at Wynn/Encore levels of aneurysm inducement. Are they trying to sell the stuff or just show off about it? Who knows? Maybe they just got confused when they developed a top-flight steakhouse and thought they needed to gouge the customer on wine to keep up appearances. On the bright side, the half-off wine nights and weekend brunch specials (unlimited champagne and Bloody Marys) atone for some of these sins. Sort of.

GET THIS: Crispy artichokes; lobster roll; crab cake; steak tartare; sweet corn soup; green asparagus soup with pea shoots; Little Gem lettuce salad; cured salmon sashimi; oysters; strip steak; flat iron steak; rib cap steak; Cowboy Ribeye; cauliflower steak; sweet corn pappardelle; broccolini; grilled sweet potato; chocolate cake; bombolini.

THILMONT

Comfortably fashionable, Andiron ups the culinary game in Summerlin, the suburb that unfortunately often proves the maxim that money can't buy good taste. I like the bar area for vino by the glass, a nice steak tartare (quail-egg yolk, thank you very much), and nutty (as in the non-kosher concept, not the flavor) Nueske-bacon-wrapped matzo balls.

B&B RISTORANTE (STRIP)   Italian

Venetian
(702) 266-9977
bandbristorante.com
5-11 p.m., daily
$75-$125

WILBURN

Of the four Batali offerings in Las Vegas, it's easy to imagine Carnevino as the flagship, because of just how well they knocked the idea of an Italian steakhouse out of the park. However, if you consider what the namesakes of B&B, Mario Batali and Joe Bastianich, became famous for, you quickly realize that this is the real heir-apparent to the original Babbo in NYC.

Both Babbo and B&B aren't so much simple Italian food, but rather fine dining done with the pallet of Italian cuisine. Batali's credo for these spots is to present the rainbow of flavors from Italy for you to paint your own picture with them. Chef Brett Uniss, a guy with a résumé boasting places like Per Se, Fatted Duck, and French Laundry, has taken the catalog of Batali classics and his own experiments and set out to rebrand B&B. They could not have chosen a better chef to do it, because the menu is looking better than ever.

All the Vegas Batali restaurants benefit from a great amount of in-house charcuterie, and the board at B&B might be the best among them. Spicy Calabrian peppers make the n'duja an addictive fatty spread, their salamis are better than almost every producer available, and the house pickles are done with terrific attention to detail. The lamb-tongue bruschetta with chanterelles will make you rethink your favorite part of a lamb's body, each of them a succulent little tender slice of meat. The menu is very pasta-heavy, taking up most of the "primi" section, but each is a terrific canvas for unique combinations of flavor. Whether it's a pork trotter ravioli with cherry tomato or rabbit confit with hen-of-the-woods mushroom on garganelli, they're all unique to the B&B experience. There's even a "pasta tasting menu" to top out on your ability to enjoy pasta in one glorious night of starch and wine—a feast fit for a pope.

The second section of the menu is where the love and work really show. The entrées follow the natural construction of a main dish; meat, starch, veg. The dishes themselves, however, almost seem like they could be at home in a fine-dining French setting! Short rib braised in Barolo wine with polenta and horseradish is one of the house favorites and one of the best examples of a dish satisfying both the higher and lower functions of human taste at once; it's incredibly savory and balanced, but also complex and exciting.

It's definitely worth saving room for dessert here, as the selection of cannolis, gelato, panna cotta, and tiramisu would make even your grandmama from the old country weep sugary tears of joy. After all that starch, meat, wine, and sweets, be sure to enjoy something from the large selection of amaros, a veritable medicine cabinet with restorative properties for anyone nearing a food coma.

GET THIS: Warm lamb tongue; house-cured salumi board; pork trotter ravioli; short rib al Barolo; rabbit porchetta; Amaretto panna cotta.

CURTAS

My feelings about B&B have vacillated over the years among loving, hating, and being completely indifferent to it. It's been mostly the latter, since they haven't changed a thing about the menu for the past nine years. But someone in the last year had the good sense to hire Brett Uniss as the Chef de Cuisine and the shot in the arm he's provided to the joint is palpable from the first bite.

BORDER GRILL (STRIP)   **Southwestern**

Mandalay Bay
(702) 632-7403
bordergrill.com
Mon.-Thurs., 11 a.m.-10 p.m.; Fri., 11 a.m.-11 p.m.;
Sat., 10 a.m.-11 p.m.; Sun., 10 a.m.-10 p.m.
$25-$75

THILMONT

For decades in Las Vegas' youngish history, the resort oasis was a veritable desert of authentic Mexican food, especially in the Tourist Corridor. Finding a dish or snack that wasn't filtered through bland Americanized tastes was about as hard to find as a useful Chihuahua pooch. But in 1999, Sin City imported some real south-of-the-border credibility—not from our troubled southern sister country, but rather from nearby Southern California. It was Border Grill, the creation of Chefs Mary Sue Milliken and Susan Feniger, who have been keeping this cuisine legit ever since at Mandalay Bay.

One of the highlights of Border Grill is its ceviche offerings, seafood cold-poached in citrus juices. Shrimp, fish, crab, and other seasonal sea-born critters are united with sweet and savories ranging from avocado and grapefruit to pickled onions and chiles. The queso fundido, a rich melty melange of Oaxacan and Spanish cheeses, is also a perennial favorite. Tacos are filled with a panoply of ingredients like grilled fish, tender lamb adobo-style, papaya, and roasted corn. Entrées are noteworthy, such as skirt steak with caramelized onions and poblano chiles and sea bass Veracruzano with capers and olives.

The true marquee of Border Grill is its famed and highly popular weekend brunch. Saturdays and Sundays are packed with revelry fueled by myriad margaritas, mojitos, and Bloody Marys. Numerous small plates are for the taking, especially the lovely green-corn tamales. Other filling dishes include plantain empanadas, huevos rancheros, and waffles with Serrano ham.

Mexican cuisine loves its sugar and Border Grill delivers well, from coconut flan and chocolate mousse to prickly pear-fruit sorbet.

To double-down for Vegas vacationers, there's also a Border Grill at the Forum Shops at Caesars Palace. *Odelay*!

GET THIS: The house guacamole; queso fundido with Oaxacan cheese and Spanish manchego; plantain empanada; all the ceviches; lamb adobo tacos; striped sea bass Veracruzano; Yucatan-style pork with achiote roasted in banana leaves; the brunch.

WILBURN

Unique Mexican is great, but the unlimited-plates weekend brunch really puts this one on the map for me. That, and the ceviche bar and happy hour.

BOUCHON (STRIP)   French

Venetian
(702) 414-6200
venetian.com
Mon.-Thurs., 7 a.m.-1 p.m.; Fri.-Sun., 7 a.m.-2 p.m.;
5-10 p.m., daily
Oyster bar 3-10 p.m., daily
$25-$75

CURTAS

Thomas Keller took some pretty big hits this year. Per Se's de-motion to two stars in the *New York Times* had the Internet (and schadenfreude-obsessed food press) all atwitter about his possibly losing his fastball. He might not be the pitcher he once was back there in Yankee Stadium, but out here in the hustings, his control is as pinpoint as ever. The epi baguettes can still blow you away from the first bite and they, like everything else on this menu, are major league. You won't find better oysters or mussels this far from an ocean, and the room is just as vibrant and comfortable as it was when it opened 13 years ago.

I've eaten here dozens of times over those years and the food—whether a special, silken, corn soup or voluptuous veal porter-house—never fails to astonish with its technical perfection and intensity. The wine list, like most in Gouge the Greenhorn Gulch, doesn't give you the courtesy of a reach-around. On the bright side, there's a nice selection of half bottles that bend you over for half the insanely inflated price. Stick with whites and light reds (think Beaujolais and vin du pays), to avoid feeling quite so violated. Those quibbles aside, asking me to choose between Bouchon and Bardot Brasserie for casual French supremacy is like asking me which one of my kids I love the most.

GET THIS: Oysters; soupe a l'oignon; corn soup (seasonal); steak frites; parfait du foie gras; moules au safran; poulet roti; truite amandine; Croque Madame; escargot; salade Lyonnaise; veal chop; boudin blanc; crème brûlée; bouchons.

THILMONT

Heading to this slice of classic Paris is a mini-adventure. Located high up in the Venezia Tower, its zinc bar, dark wood walls, huge windows, and seasonal garden patio combine for a vision of timeless refined beauty.

Many hold Bouchon dear for its morning and brunch service, and for good reason. I use an informal litmus test when judging a breakfast place: How good is its Hollandaise? As expected, Chef Thomas Keller's has the perfect viscosity (firm, but not custardy) and savoriness (a balanced lemon zestiness and not overly buttery or salty); also, on oeufs Benedict, Hobb's smoked pork loin kicks Canadian bacon's derriere back north of the border.

Of course, there's a fine dinner service of time-honored Gallic entrées like gigot d'agneau (roasted leg of lamb with chickpeas, piquillo peppers, spring onions, and lamb jus). And to top it all off is an excellent oyster bar.

CARSON KITCHEN (DOWNTOWN)   American

see map 1, page 250
124 S. Sixth Street
(702) 473-9523
carsonkitchen.com
Sun.-Wed., 11:30 a.m.-10 p.m.; Thurs.-Sat., 11:30 a.m.-11 p.m.
$25-$75

THILMONT

There's been a lot of hubbub around the "renaissance" of downtown Las Vegas over the past few years, with an influx of new restaurants catering to more contemporary foodie tastes. Some of the brouhaha has been pure media fluffernutter hype.

Carson Kitchen, however, is the legit restaurant that essentially kick-started downtown's new food scene, and it's going strong and solid. Housed in a formerly derelict mid-century motel just a block from the hustle of Fremont Street, the establishment was the brainchild of famed Kerry Simon, the charismatic and much admired "rock 'n' roll" celebrity chef. Sadly, in 2015, the culinary world lost Simon last year to illness.

What Simon set in motion is still pedal-to-the-metal at the forefront of Las Vegas' casual upscale dining universe. He was famous for riffing on American comfort food at his previous Vegas restaurants and Carson Kitchen sticks to that score. His appetizers have fervent fans, including bacon jam with baked brie and toasted baguette. And while deviled eggs are everywhere these days, his "Devil's" oeufs with crispy pancetta and caviar are most rocking. I personally go gonzo for Carson Kitchen's veal meatballs with fresh peas in a sherry-foie-gras cream sauce—as velvety as an Elvis painting.

His adaptation of the classic burger brings butter and boursin cheese to the Americana staples of cheddar, tomato, and lettuce. For my part, the jerk turkey burger is the real star. A baseball of ground gobbler is kept moist with mango chutney and slaw. It's jamming with a side of tater tots dusted with an addictive spice dust and good 'ol ketchup.

Vegetables make a nice show and can get adventurous. The restaurant's roasted beets with pistachio, orange, and goat cheese rev up a now-common side dish. Roasted rainbow cauliflower is simple with garlic and lemon. I go in for the dish of blood orange with lesser-known root vegetables—salsify, parsnip, and celery root.

With an open demonstration-style kitchen, the menu is more geared toward snacking than single-serving plates, so the entrée selection is limited. One standout is the cocoa- and espresso-dusted New York strip steak with red wine demiglace. Again, going to founder Chef Simon's sense of culinary humor is a "deconstructed" Turducken pot pie.

Lovers of sweets are treated well at Carson Kitchen, with concoctions like Bourbon fudge brownie with brown bacon butter ice cream or glazed doughnut bread pudding with rum-laced caramel and vanilla crème anglaise. The kitchen also creates its own Twinkies, if that's your gig.

Carson Kitchen is definitely a very "hip" place, but not in an annoying *poseur* sense. It's just a cool space with quality food and great mixology to boot. It gets packed fast.

GET THIS: Bacon jam with baked brie; "Devil's" oeufs with crispy pancetta and caviar; veal meatballs with peas in sherry-foie-gras cream sauce; blood oranges with root vegetables; jerk turkey burger; Bourbon fudge brownie with brown-butter bacon ice cream.

CURTAS

Kerry Simon passed away in 2015 after a lengthy illness. But he left behind a legacy of fine food and a revolution in downtown dining. What Simon wrought when he opened CK in 2014 will be felt and celebrated for years to come, but Kerry did it first and he did it best.

see map 1, page 250
3839 Spring Mtn. Road
(702) 579-0207
chadastreet.com
5 p.m.-3 a.m., daily; Mon.-Fri., 11:30 a.m.-3 p.m.
$25-$75

WILBURN

When Bank Atcharawan decided to ditch his post as wine tsar at Thai-institution Lotus of Siam to strike out on his own with Chada Thai, it wasn't entirely expected that he'd open up a place that would rival Lotus for top Thai spot in town. The smart decision he made was not to directly compete, but to fill the gaps Lotus' menu left absent. While Lotus is good for the classics, churning out mass amounts of tom kah gai to tourists all the livelong day, Chada Thai made its bones by, first, having a phenomenal, world-class, wine list that even satiates the most masterful of Master Sommeliers, and second, putting some very regional delicacies on his menu.

Chada Street took the lessons from Chada Thai and applied them with great gusto. Where Chada Thai was all the bizarre regional specialties, the Chada Street menu is all the bizarre urban specialties. This is Thai food that Thai people eat in Thai cities, when they're super busy with their Thai jobs and need to eat on their Thai streets. These secret successes don't get into the dumbed-down Western-friendly neighborhood Thai spots.

Some things are more, shall we say, "authentic," recipes of necessity that don't use the "choicest" cuts. Their tom kah gai, while super-good, uses the foot to introduce chicken. One dish is pretty much just a fried pork hock. But other than the very few misses, everything else is a dead-on bullseye hit. One of the big superstars is the moo tod nam pla, an entire bible-sized piece of pork belly marinated in fish sauce overnight, then lightly dusted in cornstarch, and they deep-fry that mamma jamma! It's served sliced up with nam prik noom, pureéd green-chile dip. Similarly mind-blowing is the kao pad mun pu, crab-fat fried rice. Crab fat? Yes, crab fat. And with a big-ass pile of crab on it, too.

To the occidental diner, nearly 90% of this menu will be alien. Despite the unusual nature of the dishes, they hold their place on the menu because in the gladiatorial ring of the various Southeast Asian food stands and trucks, they have remained victorious.

GET THIS: Yum hoi (blanched oysters with lemongrass); peak kai saap (spicy chicken wings); larb moo (ground pork with chili); koi nua (raw diced filet mignon); sai oua (northern Thai spicy sausage); tom yum nam (spicy and sour shrimp soup); duck Panang (duck curry); kao pad mun pu (crab fat fried rice); moo tod nam pla (marinated pork belly); ka moo tod (crispy pork hock); Rieslings; Gewurtztraminers; gruner veltliners; and Champagnes that go with this food like flames and a fire hose.

CURTAS

There are three great Thai restaurants in Las Vegas and two of them, sister restaurants Chada Thai and Chada Street, are only a couple of miles apart, but both go toe to toe with Lotus for Siamese supremacy. The former is more traditional Thai, while the latter is more about Thai street food, but none of that matters when your head is being blown off by one of the superb house-made curries or larb moo (ground pork with chili, onion and lime). Just as fetching (and mind blowing) are the blanched oysters with lemongrass and (lethal) bird's-eye chili, and the koi nua (raw diced filet mignon with fish sauce). I've eaten in both of these multiple times and the only reason I prefer the Street is because the wine list is deeper and the champagne list is out of this world. No cork dork worth his tartaric acid visits Vegas these days without a visit here.

The Rest of the Best

CHENGDU TASTE (WEST) — Chinese

see map 1, page 250
3950 Schiff Drive
(702) 437-7888
11 a.m.-3 p.m., 5-10 p.m.: daily
$25 or less

CURTAS

From the moment it opened, Chengdu Taste was packed. Which tells you something about the power of social media these days, and how quickly word travels when an offshoot of one of L.A.'s best Chinese restaurants opens in Vegas. The original in Alhambra was anointed one of SoCal's finest by Jonathon Gold, and that was all it took to get the Chinese cognoscenti lined up outside of this obscure location on Schiff Drive when it opened about a year ago.

Along with J&J Szechuan and Szechuan Express, Chengdu forms sort of a holy trinity of tongue-numbing eating, all of them specializing in highly spiced, take-no-prisoners Szechuan/Sichuan cooking. To eat this food is to feel like small jolts of electrons have been activated in your mouth and body, and tucking into a heaping platter of cumin lamb or won tons swimming in chili oil is a fine introduction to its pain/pleasure conundrum.

Whether it's skewers, starches, chicken in green sauce, or dandan mian (noodles), what you're getting here is the real enchilada. There's none of that "how hot do you want it?" nonsense that Thai restaurants fool with. Here you order and hang on for dear life. The beauty of this fare is that those chilies always seem to enhance the flavor of the proteins, not overwhelm them. In those dandan mian, the chewy toothsome noodles have a flavor of their own that comes through, as does the ground pork and pickled-vegetable sauce lying in the bottom of the bowl. You appreciate the individual ingredients even as the whole is exceeding the sum of its parts. All the while your eyeballs are sweating and you can't feel your lips.

Just as revelatory is "Diced Rabbit With Younger Sister's Secret Recipe," which is as bony as it is cold and coated with a fetching fermented heat. Those bones will drive you batty, but it's a real litmus test for budding gourmands who want to see what all the Sichuan shouting is about. We generally avoid hot pots (because everything ends up tasting the same), but you'll go nuts over the boiled fish in green sauce. For twenty bucks, you can get fresh fish (most likely tile fish or tilapia) that will easily feed four adults and boasts chilies from across the spectrum of heat. Those ubiquitous peppercorns wrap around your tongue, but set off, rather than obliterate, the taste and texture of the fish.

Chengdu Taste isn't our best Chinese restaurant in the sense that the high-toned mandarin-pitched Wing Lei is, but it is our most authentic. And its presence on Spring Mountain Road is further evidence of the excellence in our ever-expanding roster of Asian eateries.

P.S. For all of its popularity, table turnover is fairly fast and service is almost preternaturally quick. Our advice: Get there before noon or pick an early weeknight and you'll have no problems. The staff is bilingual and helpful and the menu is full of pretty pictures and easy to navigate. (Not always the case on Spring Mountain Road.)

GET THIS: Lamb skewers with cumin; green sauce chicken; dandan noodles; boiled fish in green sauce; shredded potato with vinegar; fried chicken with pepper; ma po tofu (tofu in chili sauce); Szechuan sautéed string bean; won ton in red chili sauce; Diced Rabbit with Younger Sister's Secret Recipe; twice-cooked pork; won ton with pepper sauce (numb taste).

THILMONT

Let's just float an important notion about dining at Chengdu Taste: This is no place for greenhorns, newbies, or those with a delicate constitution. Take the famed Szechuan peppercorns with mild anesthetic properties. Not only do they make your mouth a bit numb, they turn you into a temporary supertaster, so everything you eat holds a Boxer Rebellion on your tongue, over-punching at your taste buds. Caveat aside, this place is as legit and incendiary as it comes.

The Rest of the Best

SLS Las Vegas
(702) 761-7757
slslasvegas.com
Sun.-Thurs., 6-10:30 p.m.; Fri.-Sat., 6-11 p.m.
$25-$75

CURTAS

For a town built by Semites and other swarthy types, Las Vegas is pretty pitiful when it comes to Middle-Eastern and Mediterranean cooking. So sayeth yours truly, a swarthy Greek with more than a passing acquaintance with this food. But for a half-dozen Greek spots, a few Persian places (all marginal), and a handful of Arab or Jewish joints, a good falafel, tagine, or hummus in our humble burg is as rare as an original idea on a Guy Fieri menu. Almost every eatery with the above provenance identifies as "Mediterranean," even if the country they're cooking from is hundreds of miles from that sea. This can be confusing for someone wandering into a Persian joint expecting a gyro. The other problem is, no matter what they call themselves, the food is usually prepared with all the passion of an infomercial.

Not so at Cleo, a restaurant in a hotel (SLS) started by a guy named Nazarian—who may no longer be around (something about pesky licensing problems), but who knew a thing or two about swarthy and swashbuckling food. What Sam N. left in his wake was a solid F&B program staffed by pros who have an affinity for this cooking. And unlike all of the so-so stuff you find off the Strip, here they call their cooking "Mediterranean" without apology and without missing a beat of authenticity. Thus will you find the food of various countries surrounding (and within a few hundred miles of) the sea in question, all of it done to a turn.

No one does better mezze platters than they put out here, and expect to be blown away by the small-plates menu of babaganoush, lebneh with feta, and carrot harissa, and my Greek relatives (some of the toughest customers in the business when it comes to this cuisine) swear by the lamb kefta and the kebabs. Despite being literally all over the map, this kitchen renders faithful and upscale versions of everything from kibbeh nayyeh (Lebanese raw lamb) and merguez (North African sausage) flatbread to (Moroccan) tagines.

If I have a complaint, it's that Nazarian (a Persian by birth) didn't include more of that country's magnificent rice dishes in the mix. But speaking as one swarthy member of the tribe to another, I can forgive him this tiny transgression, because even though he left town, Sam left behind our best Middle Eastern/Mediterranean restaurant … by a mile.

GET THIS: Tagines; lebneh with feta; carrot harissa; kibbeh nayyeh; Brussels sprouts; lamb kefta; kebabs.

THILMONT

Middle Eastern cuisine (in the monolithic broad-brush sense) is so frequently cheaped-out on quality and presentation in Las Vegas, it's a shock to the system to find the gorgeous array of dishes at Cleo. From babaganoush and carrots with harissa to lamb tagine and moussaka, this cuisine shines like a jewel-encrusted genie's bottle.

CUT BY WOLFGANG PUCK (STRIP) **Steakhouse**

Palazzo
(702) 607-6300
palazzolasvegas.com / wolfgangpuck.com
5:30-11 p.m., daily
$75-$125

WILBURN

The closest thing in Vegas to being transported to the Beverly Wilshire Hotel in Beverly Hills, CUT by Wolfgang Puck became famous in L.A. as one of the main star-spotting locales of the '80s and '90s. The bait at the end of the hook that caught so many of the Hollywood elite was both the conspicuous consumption being extra conspicuous when there are paparazzi in the bushes, as well as having grub worth the hubbub.

Wolfgang Puck really put his money where his mouth is when it came to opening spots in Vegas. At one point, there were at least six of his concepts in operation in the greater metropolitan area, with CUT in no small terms the fine-dining option. Where Spago gets all the acclaim for being one of the firsts here, CUT's menu hasn't gone down in quality all these years of being set in stone. Aside from some seasonal in-and-out business, the menu is still graced by some of the steakhouse favorites pioneered at CUT Beverly Hills: beef selection where they pull around a cart of some sexy marbled cuts of Wagyu,

USDA Prime, and the lauded Snake River Farms; Indian-spiced short ribs cooked for eight mother-flippin' hours; pan-roasted Stonington Maine lobster with a black-truffle emulsion; maple-glazed pork belly with Fuji apple compote. This is the menu for Patrick Bateman, Gordon Gekko, the devil from *The Devil's Advocate*, and that cartoonishly bad French guy from the *Matrix* sequel.

It's also an impressive space for impressive people and the service certainly reflects that. Every moment your heart beats in the walls of CUT, you're the star, the executive, the mob boss—the very kind of tuchas-smooching that comes from real pros, masters of making sure you're having a good time. With that, and the kind of over-the-top finery that fits Vegas like a velvet glove, there's a reason why CUT has been a clockwork mechanism of fine steak for this many years.

GET THIS: Snake River Farms 6-oz. filet mignon; USDA Prime Nebraska corn-fed 35-day dry-aged 12-oz. ribeye; 6-oz. strip loin of the real-deal 100% pure Wagyu from Kyushu, Japan; Snake River Farms Indian-spiced short ribs.

CURTAS

As great as the steaks and seafood are, I like to swim around the appetizers and sides when I'm paddling through this menu. The wine list is not for the faint of heart or light of pocketbook.

DELMONICO STEAKHOUSE (STRIP)

Steakhouse

Venetian
(702) 414-3737
venetian.com
11:30 a.m.-2 p.m., daily
Sun.-Thurs., 5-10 p.m.; Fri.-Sat., 5-10:30 p.m.
$75-$125

CURTAS

Like a few other time-worn and treasured additions to our top 50 Las Vegas restaurants, Delmonico has been around so long we tend to take it for granted. But like Emeril's, this venerable spot is due for a salute. It opened on May 3, 1999, and for nearly 17 years has been rendering drop-dead delicious versions of the food that made Emeril Lagasse famous.

Some people call it a steakhouse, but that doesn't tell half the story. I'd argue that, on any given night, the seafood here is every bit the equal of what's served by its big sister in the MGM Grand. I'd also argue that the gumbo is a dead ringer for the Bam Man's fare in N'Awlins itself and that the lobster bisque and crispy fried oysters are as good as you'll find 1,000 miles from the Gulf of Mexico. The steaks are first rate too—especially the Nebraska-bred Piedmontese strip and the dry-aged cuts—but Executive Chef Ronnie Rainwater's apple-cured, applewood-smoked, bone-in bacon (and one of the best Caesar salads in the business) have us licking our chops every

50

time we walk in the place.

Another reason that the Big D can take a bow is that it's open for lunch, one of the few great restaurants in town that is, which makes all this gorgeous food available for those who don't want to stuff themselves after 8 p.m.

No one will ever mistake Lagasse's food for spa cuisine (his BBQ salmon comes with a "side" of potato and andouille sausage that's a meal in its own right), but he and Rainwater do spicy rib-stickin' vittles better than anyone. Equally impressive is the wine list, one of the best in the country. If super-sommelier Kevin Vogt can't find you a bottle to your liking (and in your price range), it probably doesn't exist. The cocktail bar is well-known for its concoctions and whiskeys. The booze here is so good, it makes me wish I were an alcoholic.

GET THIS: Lobster bisque; gumbo; bone-in bacon; fried oysters; BBQ salmon; Piedmontese strip steak.

WILBURN

They really do reach for the stars in everything they do here, including the expansive bar program headed by one crackerjack mixologist, Juyong Kang. Chef Ronnie Rainwater is a passionate creative chef—and has the most pleasing speaking voice I've ever heard leave a chef's mouth.

see map 1, page 250
3400 S. Jones Boulevard Suite 8
(702) 413-6868
districtonelv.com
11 a.m.-2 a.m., daily
$25 or less

CURTAS

Chef/owner Khai Vu is standing Vietnamese food on its ear and creating glamour in a cuisine that used to have all the sex appeal of Hillary Clinton. He's doing this by staying true to the idiom of the country—food rich in fresh herbs, accents, and sour fermented flavors and loaded with contrasts in both texture and aromas—but tweaking it into small sexy plates (and big soup statements) as far from the same old same old as soft shell crabs are from Mrs. Paul's fish sticks.

Take his Vietnamese carpaccio. Thinly pounded sirloin is stretched provocatively over a rectangular plate, then "marinated" in fresh lime juice and drizzled with sizzling sesame oil. The effect is at once familiar and strange; the oil and acid create a warm salad-like taste and the sliced onions and fried garlic all pop in your mouth with every bite.

Vu doesn't stop there when it comes to mixing his metaphors. Chinese bao (pork-belly buns) are getting as ubiquitous as cheeseburgers, but he gives his a Southeast Asian bent with lightly pickled daikon and carrot, micro-cilantro, and fresh roasted and crushed peanuts.

Traditional pho fans might balk, but Vu's lobster pho is worth a special trip and his yellowtail collar is worth two. Perfectly grilled, clean-tasting, soft, buttery, and succulent, it's the apotheosis of this fish, as good as any Japonaise interpretation.

Other standouts include the five-spices roasted Cornish hen and slow-braised pork belly in young coconut juice; each will have your entire table fighting for the last morsel. The groceries used here are a notch or three above District One's competitors and the cooking is more careful, more interesting, and more scrumptious than you'll find in any Vietnamese restaurant in the Mojave Desert.

We used to think all Vietnamese food tasted alike, until Khai Vu showed up on the scene to re-interpret it for us. Even better, he's opened a downtown branch—called Le Pho—where his tasty takes on banh mi, vermicelli bowls, and hoi nan chicken rice are becoming legends in their own right.

GET THIS: Lobster pho; carpaccio of beef; Hue spicy beef noodle soup; the Big Bone soup; bao pork-belly buns; five-spice roasted Cornish game hen; beef and lemongrass wrapped in betel leaves; grilled whole squid; slow-braised pork belly in coconut juice; clay-pot chicken rice.

THILMONT

The day-to-day go-to here is the unctuous oxtail fried rice. There's also the eye-popping live Maine lobster pho with a whole carapace "crawling" out of the steamy bowl. The eatery sources a good seasonal selection of not-so-common seafood, such as razor clams and sea snails. The five-spice Cornish hen is a snappy little clucker, too.

The Rest of the Best

see map 2, page 251
3555 S. Town Center Drive, Suite 105
(702) 586-6500
dueforni.com
11 a.m.-10 p.m., daily
$25-$75

CURTAS

Two ovens. One for thin and crispy Roman-style pizzas, the other for the puffier, chewier, Neapolitan kind. Both made with superb ingredients, house-made sausages, and more care than you'll find in any other suburban Italian restaurant. The man behind it all is Carlos Buscaglia—formally trained, Strip-seasoned—a man who has a Midas touch with pastas and pizza.

Everyone starts with the turkey meatballs (polpette) and beef carpaccio (ingeniously wrapped around arugula greens), but we're nuts about his salads (Caesar, panzanella, spinach, beets) as well. Even this noted beets hater finds a lot to like when Carlos roasts the little buggers and dresses them with basil pesto and fig vincotto.

If you haven't guessed by now, Due Forni is as far from a neighborhood Italian/pizza joint as Lake Como is from Lake Mead. This is sleek and sophisticated Italian fare, served in a comfortable laid-back setting, at prices that won't break the bank. Pastas like semolina gnocchi with smoked bacon and peas and penne Bolognese are worthy of hushed tones, white table cloths, and fancy china. Here, you get them amidst families, casualness, and cacophony. A lively bar scene also sets the tone, as does a late-night crowd of industry regulars. All come for the cocktails and one of the best wine programs in any restaurant off the Strip. What it lacks in size, it makes up for in quality juice that's priced to sell, not to please some accountant.

Small but mighty is a good description of Due Forni, its menu, and its wine list. It's not just the best pizza in town, it also may be our best Italian restaurant. It also has the good sense to bring in all of its gelatos from Desyree Alberganti's Gelatology, so you'll never go wrong here at the end of your meal, either.

GET THIS: Carpaccio; polpette; smoked pork belly with blueberries; polpio (roasted octopus); beet salad; Caesar salad; panzanella (bread) salad; mozzarella bar; Chef's Platter (salumi and cheese); semolina gnocchi; penne Bolognese; ravioli with ricotta and roasted mushrooms; roasted branzino (sea bass); sirloin steak; flat iron steak; pizza Margherita; pizza tartufo; Due Forni pizza; pizza picante; gelato.

THILMONT

This is one of the true treasures of Summerlin dining. It's an elegant but refined space, perfect for indulging in a short rib panino, a "Tartufo" pizza redolent with truffle crema, or a lovely lasagna. The west side of the Las Vegas Valley needs more dining establishments (of any cuisine) like this one. Now!

MGM Grand
(702) 891-7374
emerilsrestaurants.com
11:30 a.m.–10 p.m., daily
$75-$125

THILMONT

Chef Emeril Lagasse is one of the patron saints of modern Las Vegas cuisine. His mainstay at the MGM Grand, Emeril's New Orleans Fish House, has been serving visitors and locals for 22 years now. Placed in the thrumming heart of the original megacasino, the restaurant brings in daily some of Las Vegas' finest seafood.

The best way to start dinner at Emeril's is to splurge on the impressive seafood platter. It arrives multi-tiered and crammed with shucked oysters, littleneck clams, Creole-boiled shrimp, scallop ceviche, snow crab legs, spicy tuna tartare, and citrusy Australian lobster tail segments. Obligatory ramekins of cocktail sauce, remoulade, and Champagne mignonette are at the side for dipping.

Fish always means soups and stews and Lagasse has a luscious sweet-corn and Maine lobster bisque and a Louisiana-style crustacean and andouille-sausage gumbo. And while Emeril is largely associated with New Orleans where he first came to fame, he also does great tribute to his Massachusetts origin with hearty Fall River-style clam chowder. An abundant selection of salads includes a steakhouse-style baby iceberg wedge slathered in bacon, tomato, bleu, ranch, and red onions. The seafood salad unites shrimp, crab, and lobster with a vintage Green Goddess dressing blessing.

Hot dishes for sharing venture into Bayou Country: frog legs fried in Crystal-brand hot sauce; alligator meatballs with remoulade; down-home crawfish étouffée; and barbecued shrimp with biscuits and mussels in green curry sauce.

Signature main courses include barbecued salmon with andouille sausage, pecan-crusted redfish with pepperjack cheese, and seared scallops with smoked bacon. Or try ribeye with trinity vegetables, pan-seared beef tenderloin with wild mushrooms, and a double-cut pork chop with chived-smashed potatoes and sautéed kale.

The pièce de résistance of Emeril's, and my personal favorite, is the lavish dish of baked Australian cold-water lobster tail with trumpet mushrooms, roasted tomatoes, and truffled cream sauce under a crust of buttered crumbs. It's a new-style lobster Thermidor that's somewhat light, but also astoundingly sumptuous. At market price, it's also serious cash in a chafing dish.

The Crescent City is a dessert town, and the strawberry-rhubarb crisp, pecan pie, carrot cake, bread pudding, and the house-favorite banana cream pie are for the toffee-toothed diner.

Especially handy are a satisfying lunch service and a good happy hour. Indeed, the whole shebang is trademarked "bam!"

GET THIS: Chilled seafood platter; charred Spanish octopus; lobster bisque; Fall River clam chowder; barbecued salmon; ribeye steak; baked Australian lobster tail; banana cream pie.

WILBURN

In a cuisine where 99% of the restaurants opt for the same dusty recipes and corny name-brand placement, Emeril's Fish House is a beacon of hope. In the same way that Bardot doesn't just do French staples, Emeril's actually takes the rich building blocks of Louisiana Gulf food and really "kicks it up a notch." Bam!

ESTIATORIO MILOS (STRIP)

Cosmopolitan
(702) 698-7000
cosmopolitanlasvegas.com
Sun.-Thurs., noon-11 p.m.; Fri.-Sat., noon-midnight
$75-$125

THILMONT

Estiatorio Milos is a Greek restaurant, plain and simple, but then some.

First, throw the memory of your hometown Hellenic hack shack out of your mind's Acropolis window. This isn't scraggly lamb shank and lame souvlaki. No, this is spectacular! Greek cuisine, in its historical perfection, is unfortunately unheralded, especially in North America where many merely think of gyros. Indeed, the Greeks taught the Romans how to cook, eventually turning peasant gruel into the Italian cuisine so lauded today worldwide.

Estiatorio Milos is the Las Vegas outpost of a Montreal-founded restaurant city-state that rescues a cuisine beleaguered by hot lamps and languishing service and returns it to its fine true form. Foremost, it's a temple to fresh fish, much of it flown in from the Mediterranean. Ordered by the pound, diners will find a rotating roster of seasonal catches, including loup de mer, Dorado royale, Dover sole, and blue lobster. Most are simply grilled with lemon and olive oil.

Also from the sea is a Poseidon-worthy adventure at the oyster bar, including fresh bivalves, tuna tartare, and even avgotaraho, that lusty-salty expert-eater experience that is cured mullet roe.

Keeping it real with epic Homeric feasts, there are lamb shanks served with Greek-style potatoes—a mint-and-dill-laden relatively modern invention. Also good are the ribeye and filet mignon.

Of course, Milos serves familiar traditional sides, like the Greek salad, bursting with tomatoes and barrel-aged feta cheese. A platter of grilled vegetables comes with minted yogurt and springy Haloumi cheese. Indeed, the bursting plate of lightly fried calamari is Promethean in illuminating the appetizer. Don't forget the taramosalata, tzatziki, and skordlia, either.

With all these dinner dishes at hand, Estiatorio Milos has a lunch service that's perhaps even more famed. It's certainly one of the best upscale midday-repast deals on the entire Vegas Strip. For a price in the $25 range, you get three courses. The appetizer flight can be a mezze plate, smoked salmon on a bagel, tomato salad, grilled octopus, or crab cakes. The main course can be Mediterranean sea bass, Atlantic salmon, shrimp, lamb chops, or lobster pasta. Some of the more lofty items have an upcharge. Dessert choices, such as thick yogurt and seasonal fruit, are Platonically ideal.

GET THIS: Greek salad; grilled vegetables; Milos Special fried zucchini; Greek bottarga; Maryland crab cake; sardines; the Carabinieros (langoustines); Milokopi (sea bass in salt crust); Greek fried potatoes; whatever fish your wallet can afford; lamb chops; lunch special.

CURTAS

The best fish in town, period. Also, the best Greek food in town by a Peloponnesian mile. You'll pay through the nose, but you'll also be shouting "Opa!" with every bite. Let the sommeliers guide you to some fabulous Greek white wines at some relatively gentle prices. Come for the $25 lunch if you're on a budget.

see map 1, page 250
4480 Paradise Road
(702) 364-5300
ferraroslasvegas.com
Mon.-Fri., 11:30 a.m.-2 a.m.; Sat.-Sun., 4 p.m.-2 a.m.
$75-$125

WILBURN

A Calabrian family-run institution, Ferraro's Italian Restaurant &
Wine Bar has been around since the days when spaghetti and meatballs were considered exotic. The food has thankfully undergone
the same changes as most other cuisines and the owners have taken
their diners' willingness to try new things as a challenge. Ferraro's is
quite possibly the most labor-intensive Italian spot in Vegas, and as
such, the greatest deal. It's the kind of food to which PBS specials
would be dedicated—with lots of slow-mo shots and Vivaldi violin
solos.

The menu—including specials, happy hours, educational lun-
cheons, holidays, late nights, and wine dinners—is ponderous. That
said, it's not full of rote repetition, a couple different topping and
pasta combos; rather, it shows the family's remarkable range. On
one end of the spectrum, they introduce some really rustic gener-
ations-old recipes. In fact, the Calabrian specialty of trippa satriano
is one of their specialties and I don't think tripe has been made this

well in Vegas at any other time. The usually barnyard-scented chewy folds are cleansed with multiple rounds of lemon-salt scrubs and overnight soaks, rinsing out the essence of the cow bile that sack held when it was living. It's done in a spicy sauce (Calabrians love their spice), soaked up by the porous tender tripe. It's a dish for people who'd never eat tripe.

Most of the pastas are made in-house; not that they'd brag, they just love the quality. Their kitchen prep starts early in the morning and ends late into the night. They even employ the secret to making great tortellini (when you're lucky enough to get them): a little old grandma who comes in once a week and cranks out a massive batch of them. Don't ask me why; it's some kind of wisdom that sweet old ladies inherit and no one else can copy.

Ferraro's under-promises and over-delivers, in a category of red-tablecloth Italian that all too often does the opposite.

GET THIS: Trippa satriano; tortellini; osso buco; coniglio brasato; gnocchi pomodoro; polpettine (meatballs); Apulian burrata with mushrooms and artichoke; carpaccio; house-made sausage; spaghettini aglio e olio; manzo tonnato; risotto; braised rabbit; pappardelle mimmo; tiramisu; lots and lots of red wine.

CURTAS

An Italian Renaissance of sorts took place a couple of years ago, when Gino and Mimmo Ferraro had the good sense to put Francesco Di Caudio in the kitchen. In making this move, they turned their restaurant, which had been good for decades, into one that's great. Fabulous wine (one of the best Italian lists in the country) and warm family-run hospitality have always been the watchwords here, but with Di Caudio's food leading the way, Ferraro's has catapulted to the top rung of our pasta palaces.

Everyone gets the osso buco (which is definitive), but the way to go is to put yourself in the chef's hands and let him dazzle you with an array of antipasti, contorni, primi, and secondi piatti that take a back seat to no other chef's.

GLUTTON (DOWNTOWN) American

see map 1, page 250
616 E. Carson Avenue
(702) 366-0623
gluttonlv.com
Tues.-Fri., 10 a.m.-2:30 p.m.; Sat.-Sun., 9 a.m.-3 p.m.;
Tues.-Thurs., 4:30-9:30 p.m.; Fri., 4:30-10 p.m.; Sat., 5-10 p.m.;
Sun., 5-9:30 p.m.
$25-$75

CURTAS

When Bradley Manchester announced he'd be opening a small restaurant in downtown Las Vegas in 2014, you could hear the guffaws all the way to Red Rock Station, his former employer where he toiled away for years as executive chef for the entire hotel. Manchester's background had always been in running large multi-venue concepts and nothing in his résumé gave even the slightest hint that he might be capable of pulling off the sort of chef-driven jewel-box he planted smack dab on the corner of Carson and Seventh. Glutton is a mere block away from Carson Kitchen, his competition, but also, no doubt, his inspiration, and between the two of them, downtowners (and a fair number of tourists) now pack the joints day and night for food that downtown Las Vegas, a restaurant wasteland for decades, couldn't imagine even a few years ago.

Manchester's strong suit, like CK's, is a limited menu of very personal dishes done to a fare-thee-well, such as Buffalo-style sweetbreads (yes, thymus glands that taste like chicken wings), house-made Parker rolls (addictive), veggies done so ingeniously—wood-fired curried cauliflower, shaved Brussels sprouts—they could make a vegan out of you. If proteins are what you seek, you should start with the burger (perhaps Vegas' best bit o' beef) or a wood-roasted half-chicken with cheddar jalapeño biscuits you'll be unable to stop eating. Shrimp or sea bream come out of that same oven and are every bit as good as anything on the Strip, at quite a softer price. Downtown Las Vegas is booming these days, and its best restaurant is keeping things that way.

GET THIS: Parker House rolls; curried cauliflower; spicy pork rinds; anything wood-fired; Glutton burger; Buffalo-style sweetbreads; lamb crépinettes; brown-butter gnocchi; caramel-corn profiteroles; apple and olive oil upside-down cake.

THILMONT

I'll admit to not being a fan of the rotund signage. That being said, Glutton does offer some of the best cuisine downtown in the gastropuby vein. Think wood-charred broccoli, Barolo-braised beef cheeks, and chocolate bread pudding.

Caesars Palace
(702) 731-7286
caesarspalace.com
Wed.-Sun., 5:30-9:30 p.m.
$125 and up

CURTAS

For the first four editions of this book (and for the last 10 years), Restaurant Guy Savoy has been one of the top two restaurants in Las Vegas, and, without a doubt, one of the top 10 restaurants in all of the United States. So why are we "demoting" it this year to mere "Essential 50" status?

Two reasons: One, it lost Mathieu Chartron this year as its executive chef, and two, it lost Mathieu Chartron as its executive chef.

If you're familiar with the Michelin Guide, you know that whenever a starred restaurant loses its top chef (to death, retirement, or whatever), the guidebook immediately takes a star away from it—not as a criticism or demotion, but as a show of respect for the departing chef and his cooking. *Eating Las Vegas* is fully aware that the food at GS was not Chartron's. We know the recipes here (as well as those at Joël Robuchon and Twist by Pierre Gagnaire) are products of corporate vetting and testing way back in France. But they still have to be executed with passion and precision, every night, 6,000 miles from where they were conceived. To say that Chartron did this, and maintained Savoy's impeccably high standards, is an understatement. We have no doubt new chef Julien Asseo will eventually prove equal to the task, but until he gets his sea legs under him, we will bid a tearful farewell to chef Chartron and content ourselves with the best bread cart in the business.

We look forward to seeing how Asseo fills the big shoes that were left behind. (As of this writing, we've only sampled his food once, which isn't enough to take the full measure of the place.) In the meantime, we'll quench our thirst from one of the world's great wine lists, which has quite a few bargains if you're willing to hunt for them.

GET THIS: Langoustines three ways; colors of caviar; mosaic of milk-fed poulard with foie gras and artichoke; artichoke and black-truffle soup; lobster salad; salmon iceberg; turbot a la plancha; veal three ways; roasted duck breast "mustard crust;" pan-seared quails; Menu Classique; Menu Inspiration; the bread cart; the cheese cart; the petit fours cart; the champagne cart; and the wine. Always the wine. Always French.

WILBURN

In the Holy Trinity of Haute French in Vegas, Guy Savoy would be The Son, a place of freeform vigor and experimentation on one side of the menu and the stone-written classics on the other. Which is better? Such is the mystery, and the delight.

The Rest of the Best

THE GOODWICH (DOWNTOWN)

American

see map 1, page 250
Soho Lofts,
900 S. Las Vegas Blvd. #120
(702) 910-8681
thegoodwich.com
Mon.-Fri., 7 a.m.-10 p.m.;
Sat.-Sun., 8 a.m.-10 p.m.
$25 or less

WILBURN

When you say that a sandwich joint at the bottom of a condo building is among the top 50 restaurants in Las Vegas, you invite a level of, let's say, scrutiny. When you see something like that in some trendy L.A. or NYC mag, touting a spot that's making "this totally authentic (insert obscure ethnic dish)," you can almost bet it's some hipster self-gratifying wankfest—using bottom-of-the-barrel ingredients and likely more than a few jarred Sysco sauces. I want to stress with the utmost sincerity that The Goodwich belongs in the top 50 and a point could be argued for it being in the top half of it.

In their original location, a small shack in front of a dive bar, they knocked expectations out of the park all day long. Now with an actual kitchen and dining room, they're even better.

The Goodwich promises nothing more than "stacked-rite" sandwiches and it delivers art between two slices of bread. The menu, comprised of classics redone with fine-dining dedication, is highly geared toward seasonally driven recipes. In the summer, they use perfect tomatoes in a simple $4.50 sandwich or fresh sweet corn in their "street-corn" sandwich, done elotes-style with lime crema, goat ricotta, and grilled zucchini.

You could say that their sandwiches fall into two categories: perfected classics and original experiments. The classics are easy to spot: a cold brown here, a patty melt there, a fried egg if you like.

Though classic, they don't escape The Goodwich's single-minded perfectionism, as even the corned beef is house-cured, the cream cheese is smoked, and the butter was chosen after thorough research. These sandwiches kick even big-money celebrity-driven spots square in the groin, but the originals—oh, the originals, my friends—are truly something to behold. The seasonal street corn I mentioned is a stand-out winner among them, but the choice becomes so much more Sophie'd when you have to decide against a pâté de champagne sandwich or the rotating Pig o' the Week, or the Sea Smoke of smoked whitefish and remoulade. Or the ham sandwich with mostarda. O-o-or literally anything they've ever put between bread.

Their non-sandwich offerings are equally beautiful. The breakfast menu has a few sandwiches in the same vein as their regular menu (albeit with more egg and grits), but they also have baked hash, grapefruit brûlée, or some truly amazing pastries—their bacon blondies with thyme caramel are a high note. This might be the only spot in the Top 50 with a one-dollar-sign rating on Yelp, so gamble a tenner and be utterly amazed.

GET THIS: Ham & (on rye); Sea Smoke (on white); Street Corn (on monte cristo'd white); patty melt (on rye); pâté de champagne; tomato (on white); a bag of chicken skins on the side.

CURTAS

I wrote last year that I can only get so excited about a sandwich shop, but there are so many good sandwiches in downtown Las Vegas right now that I decided to get a lot more excited about them. The Goodwich may be the first among equals and its hand-tooled sammies and salads get your attention from the first bite. As much as I admire their craftsmanship and use of good groceries, I wish the service was a little faster and that they played with their breads a bit more (as in offering a more interesting selection). Slow service is the price you pay for these hand-made beauties, but the bread, although always fresh, is also a bit boring. Still, the Patty (a riff on the classic patty melt with smoked cream cheese oozing into the beef) is so good you'll forgive all misdemeanors.

HARVEST BY ROY ELLAMAR **American**

Bellagio
(702) 693-8865
bellagio.com
5-10 p.m.; daily
$75-$125

When Bellagio opened in 1998, the set of restaurants filling the world's most expensive hotel were game-changing. Some of them grace this very list even today and rightfully so. Sensi was part of the phase-two expansion in 2004 and never really broke into stride like the big-name places that drew famous New York chefs. A baker's-dozen years later, the bigwigs upstairs thought they could do better business in that spot and pulled the plug. But then, something amazing happened: They didn't screw everything up horribly for once! The nearly $1 million transformation of the beautiful but oft-overlooked space kept the giant rock slabs and turned the kitchen into a kind of stage terrarium. Best of all, they handed the reins over to the man who had been running Sensi the several years prior and turned it into Harvest by Roy Ellamar.

The Sensi space could have become some trendy fast-casual concept by an absent or completely fabricated celebrity chef or, God forbid, yet another culinary fart joke from Guy Fucking Fieri. Instead,

Roy Ellamar got the restaurant he deserved: a place where small artisanal farms are a priority, not a buzzword, and where his open globe of cuisine could flourish. When I first dined at Harvest, I said that it was Chef Roy's moment, the same moment as when Batali opened Babbo or Daniel Boulud stepped into the kitchen of Le Cirque in Manhattan. That's a sentiment I stand by today.

Harvest has a menu that you can tell was fun to brainstorm. Foie gras and duck confit sliders, farro porridge, Brussels sprouts with barrel-aged maple, a rotating (literally) section of rotisserie slow-cooked foods—the list goes on. Not to mention that the dining room has two roaming carts: one for dessert and one "snack wagon." The snack wagon dispenses bite-sized portions of things Chef Roy has been experimenting with and this is a chance to see how they sell and get a little feedback on them, a beta test if you will. In fact, chefs from around Vegas, as well as a few mixologists, have commandeered this cart for a night or two to work the room and try out something new or fun on the guests.

The size or diversity or uniqueness of the menu isn't necessarily the draw, but rather the dedication to going above and beyond in terms of sourcing. It's even gone to the point that Chef Roy worked with corporate to get these small farms terrific contracts for MGM Resorts' whole family of casinos, so that they can survive to supply his microgreens, herbs, super-locavore tomatoes, and other seasonals. I'd honestly be surprised if they even stocked a can opener in his kitchen, that's how seriously they are about making their food only with ingredients that have felt the tender loving care of Chef Roy himself.

GET THIS: Duck confit sliders; Brussels sprouts; rotisserie porchetta; farro porridge; steak tartare; fisherman's stew; sashimi; rock shrimp tempura; lamb chops.

CURTAS

A huge restaurant in a giant casino with a menu that feels like it comes from some finely-tuned neighborhood gastropub? Yep, that's what Roy Ellamar has created with this Bellagio re-boot. Somehow he manages to pull off everything from sashimi with bourbon-aged ponzu to rock shrimp tempura (and one of the best steak tartares in town). I'm partial to his small plates, but the fisherman's stew and marinated lamb chops are nothing to sneeze at, either.

The Rest of the Best

HEARTHSTONE KITCHEN & CELLAR (WEST) American

Red Rock Resort
(702) 797-7344
hearthstonelv.com
Sun.-Thurs., 5-10 p.m.; Fri.-Sat., 5-11 p.m.;
Brunch: Sun., 11 a.m.-3 p.m.
$25-$75

THILMONT

These are great days for roasted and fired viands in Las Vegas. Going beyond classic steakhouses, a new breed of restaurant is bringing the butcher's chop shop into the dining space itself. Hearthstone Kitchen & Cellar, located at Red Rock Resort in Summerlin, is one of the highlights of serious meatery in Vegas. Hearthstone is led by Chef Brian Massie, a New Yorker who infuses the refined gourmet spirit of Brillat-Savarin into a menu that would thrill a camp of famished lumberjacks.

Appetizers are abundant, including braised-beef short-rib meatballs, Dungeness crab cake, and spicy lollipop chicken wings. I especially enjoy the baked ricotta with truffled honey, Gouda, and black pepper. The deviled eggs are quite good. Charcuterie is definitely a thing here. Chef Massie has assembled a larder of dozens of meats and cheeses to be sliced and served, from beef bresaola and duck prosciutto to Beecher's Flagship Reserve and Point Reyes toma. Plus, housemade pork rillette and country terrine are ready to be lavishly spread on bread.

With a convivial atmosphere conducive to gourmand-style partying, a half-dozen flatbreads are wood-fired, including the kingly Abe Froman with fennel-garlic sausage and mushroom with fromage blanc and Gouda.

Entrées are substantial, including rotisserie chicken with rocket salad, roasted tomatoes, and preserved lemon; pan-seared salmon with eggplant, chickpeas, and herbed yogurt; and grilled hanger steak with fries and truffled aioli. The main attraction, though, is Massie's Whole Beast Feast—a call-ahead banquet of crispy-skinned suckling pig, sour mustard, preserved apple butter, and country bread.

Hearthstone also has a robust Sunday brunch, as befitting a casino eatery. It's à la carte ordering, from eggs Benedict made with upscale Benton's ham to huevos rancheros with house red chili sauce. As many diners are hankering for chicken and waffles these days, Chef Massie steps it up to duck confit on whole-wheat-rye griddled bases. Kale and quinoa salads befit a place decked out in modern-rustic décor. And a mighty Bloody Mary tableside cart can be ordered for groups.

Finally, if all that's not enough, there's even a kid's menu.

GET THIS: Deviled eggs; Dungeness crab cake; beef-short-rib meatballs; duck prosciutto; rotisserie chicken; hanger steak; roasted suckling pig dinner; huevos rancheros; kale salad.

CURTAS

Brian Massie and his company seem to be opening restaurants faster than I can eat in them, but for the last couple of years whenever I'm on the west side of town, I've been content to take all my meals at his flagship. Were it not for Hearthstone (and Salute, its solid sister ship next door), I would've written off the Red Rock casino a long time ago. But Massie and his crew have resuscitated the food quality here with excellent wood-fired pizzas, serious salads and soups (don't miss the shaved Brussels sprout "Caesar"), and chef-driven fare the likes of which you don't usually see 15 miles from the Strip. The beauty of Hearthstone is you can treat it like a watering hole, a sports bar, or a serious restaurant, depending on your mood. They even do a half-off Monday-night wine thing that packs the place with serious (or at least semi-serious) oenophiles.

HIROYOSHI JAPANESE CUISINE (WEST)   Japanese

see map 1, page 250
5900 W. Charleston Boulevard #10
(702) 823-2110
hiroyoshi702.com
5-9:30 p.m., daily; Thurs. & Fri., 11:30 a.m.-2 p.m.
$25-$75

CURTAS

The latest in our wave of edomae sushi restaurants is, by far, the farthest from the economic eating engine that is Spring Mountain Road. By several miles, in fact. Hiroyoshi is in such an obscure place for a restaurant of its quality that you have to question the sanity of one Hiro Yoshi, a former sushi chef at Blue Ribbon, for taking over the space to begin with. But any doubts you have as to his state of mind will evaporate the moment after you take your first bite. Bear in mind, this is Tokyo-style sushi. The real deal. Fine fish, finely cut, and served on rice so pure, you can count the grains in your mouth.

Don't even bother to show up if you're the sort who eschews fresh fish for overwrought inside-out sushi rolls. Being no fool, Hiro-san includes some specialty rolls on his menu (unlike Yui and Kabuto), so here you can get a Dragon Maki Mega Roll, if that's your bag. But the reason to seek out this place is Hiro-san's knife work, and to eat impeccable fresh fish on even more impeccably seasoned rice. Or to enjoy an umami-bomb of grilled cod with mushrooms or unagi

72

(eel) stuffed tamago (egg), or to watch him compose his drop-your-chopsticks, intricate, sashimi plate. For the truly adventurous among you are also chewy gelatinous strands of jellyfish, containing more texture than taste, which will bolster your street cred among the "bizarre-foods" crowd. All of it is part of an $85/pp omakase that stands up to anything Yui or Kabuto can throw at you and puts most sushi on the Strip to shame.

Put it all together and you have a neighborhood sushi bar that feels like it relocated from Shibuya. The fact that it exists at all, and seems to be thriving, is a testament to how far our Japanese eating has come. About the only thing to criticize is the size of the (very limited) sake list. But in a 30-seat restaurant, there's only so much room for storage. Just like in the teeny tiny sushi bars of Tokyo.

GET THIS: Chef's omakase; sashimi plate; tempura platter.

THILMONT

A total gem, even if it's not located in the thrumming heart of Chinatown or the Strip. Beyond the high-quality omakase wonders at pretty much bargain prices, don't pass up non sushi/sashimi items, such as sunamuno salad with seafood and a grilled quintet of Japanese mushrooms.

JOEL ROBUCHON (STRIP)

French

MGM Grand
(702) 891-7925
mgmgrand.com
5:30-10 p.m., daily
$125 and up

CURTAS

What Joël Robuchon has done for Las Vegas has been immeasurable. When he opened his doors at the MGM in 2005, *Gourmet* magazine editor Ruth Reichl called it the most significant restaurant event of the (then-young) century. Robuchon single-handedly focused the world's attention on the Las Vegas restaurant scene and gave it a legitimacy that all the steakhouses and Le Cirques couldn't bestow. He thus began a French Revolution that culminated in Guy Savoy and Pierre Gagnaire planting their flags here and raised the level of cooking up and down Las Vegas Boulevard in the process.

One of the ways he did this was by placing Claude Le Tohic at the helm. French chefs don't come any more honored or respected and Le Tohic was in the kitchen every day for 10 years, sending out plate after plate of astonishing perfection. But all good things must come to an end, and Claude moved on this year (to San Francisco). Now, we're left to wonder if such an operation can sustain the same level of excellence. We're also wondering if it's possible to replace a Hall of Famer of Le Tohic's caliber and how the hotel will justify these prices ($455 for 16 courses) in the process.

Will you have a wonderful meal here? Yes. Will you be surrounded by comped high-rollers and trophy-hunting tourists? Absolutely. Most importantly, will you be eating the food of Joël Robuchon, developed by his team in Paris, then translated and shipped across the pond to young lieutenants still in need of a lot of seasoning? *Mais oui*, as the French would say. Stick with the shorter menus (priced between $127 and $250/pp), avoid the wine list (unless someone else is paying), and by all means, fill up on bread (and butter).

GET THIS: Le caviar (oscetra caviar with king crab on a crustacean gelée); L'oursin (sea urchin atop fennel); La Langoustine (truffled langoustine with simmered green cabbage); Le Saumon (salmon confit coated with caviar and wasabi cream); Le Homard, lobster any way they're making it; L'oeuf de Caille Miroir (pan-fried egg with black truffle); La Langouste (spiny lobster with green curry); Le Black Cod; Le Boeuf (Chateaubriand for two "Rossini"-style); the bread; the cheese; and the butter. Don't forget the butter.

WILBURN

The reputation this restaurant and chef hold is not unearned; the term "fine dining" doesn't fully express the perfection and obsessive quality that take place in this kitchen. Every single element your senses can register about what occurs beyond those convex glass doors is honed to a razor edge, every ingredient the absolute pinnacle of what's available. This is more like a private personalized art installation than a restaurant, and you eat the masterpieces!

KABUTO EDOMAE SUSHI (WEST)   Japanese

see map 1, page 250
5040 W. Sring Mtn. Road Suite 4
(702) 676-1044
kabutolv.com
6 & 8:30 p.m. seatings, daily
$75-$125

CURTAS

Kabuto is too good for you. That's what I say to most people who ask me where to find "good sushi" when what they're fishing for is the sort of flabby over-wrought frippery that gave it a bad name. Stop reading right now if you're the sort who goes gaga over all-you-can-eat anything, or if you've ever swooned over a spider roll, or if you've ever craved a California roll. If you're that person, there's nothing I can do other than feel sorry for you. But if you enjoy the real deal—pristine hand-carved slices of exquisite swimmers atop barely warm seasoned rice—then we've got something to talk about.

Real sushi, Edomae (Tokyo-style) sushi, is a relatively new phenomenon. It's only been around a couple of hundred years in Japan and for about three in Vegas. "Edo" is the ancient Japanese word for Tokyo, and it refers to sushi served by the piece, in a serene setting, with mildly vinegared rice and the slightest dab of true wasabi (not that bright green horseradish stuff they smear on in Americanized joints). True sushi can and should be eaten with the fingers. You dip only the fish, ever-so-delicately into the soy, making sure not to sully the rice with all that salt, then pop the whole thing in your mouth. If all of this sounds like an edible form of performance art, congratulations, you're starting to get it.

Real sushi bars are all about the subtle interplay among raw food, minimalist preparation, the chef, and the customer. They're not about stuffing your face with some inside-out screaming-or-gasm roll containing more ingredients than an episode of "Game of Thrones." If you want to eat sushi like a pro, take a seat and go either the Nigiri Omakase ($48 and perfect for beginners) or the Yoroi (intermediate, $80) route. The first one gets you only sliced fish on rice of the highest pedigree, while the second throws in sashimi and faultless grilled items for some variety.

Serious sushi hounds go whole hog with the Kabuto menu ($120) that expands all categories and will keep you nailed to your seat with fascination. Sake, the only thing to drink with this food, is expensive by the bottle and gently priced by the carafe. Anyone who drinks red wine with this food should commit seppuku on the spot.

GET THIS: Nigiri Omakase; Yoroi Omakase; Kabuto Omakase; sake by the carafe.

WILBURN

Edomae sushi requires a massive amount of stress and detail for something so minimalistic, and Kabuto does not shirk that duty. An extremely curated experience, as long as your ass is in a seat, some of the finest fish in town will be in front of you.

see map 2, page 251
9340 W. Sahara Avenue
Suite 106
(702) 671-0005
khouryslv.com
Sun.-Thurs., 11 a.m.-10 p.m.;
Fri.-Sat., 11 a.m.-11 p.m.
$25 or less

CURTAS

We have long admired Khoury's, the Mediterranean/Lebanese restaurant formerly located in the far southwest reaches of the valley. The only thing we didn't like about it was how far it was from our house. Now, it's a bit closer (on West Sahara), having relocated in the past year, and the only thing not to love is how it will spoil you for all other Las Vegas versions of this cuisine. Be forewarned: This city is full of not-so-great Greek/Mediterranean restaurants—a surprising number of which are run by Russians—and industrial gyro meat and tepid tabbouleh are pretty much standard-issue in the 'burbs.

But Khoury's is straight from the old county, in all the best ways. All sausages, pickles, sauces, and pita are made from scratch and the food is aggressively spiced just like they do on the Mediterranean. The house mezze sampler is a nice way to start, and a nice way to feed four-to-six hungry souls. It's so chock full of goodness (and about a dozen vegetable dishes), you may forget about eating your spiced, ground-meat, kafta kebabs or the wonderful whole roasted chicken.

Much to the chagrin of my relatives, no Greek in town can top what Khoury's does with fantastic falafel, heavenly hummus, smoky babaganoush, delightful dolmades, luscious loubieh (green beans with garlic and tomatoes), and all sorts of mashed and seasoned cheeses, yogurt, and vegetables. Through it all, you'll be sopping things up with the never-ending baskets of puffy pita—so light, nutty, and addictive you'll inhale two or three of these Mesopotamian marvels as they get replenished to your table straight from the oven. Try not to fill up on bread, and don't miss the sujuk (spicy sausage) pizza, or lahm bi ajeen (ground lamb pizza), either.

That all of this is done in-house, at easy-to-digest prices (almost everything on the menu is well under twenty bucks, except for the meats), is remarkable. That food can taste this good and be so good for you is a blessing from the food gods.

GET THIS: Lahm bi ajeen; sujuk pizza; tabbouleh; hummus; loubieh (green beans); labni-matoon; mtabal baba ganoush (fresh grilled eggplants); mezza platters; bamieh (sautéed okra); whole roasted chicken; dolmades; kafta kebabs; pita bread. Lots and lots of pita bread.

THILMONT

The mezze platter alone is reason enough to dine at Khoury's. I can't get enough of that lanbi (yogurt cheese in olive oil), loubieh, and fresh puffy pita! If it had a real lounge, it would be perfect.

LOTUS OF SIAM (EAST)

see map 1, page 250
953 E. Sahara Avenue
Suite A5
(702) 735-3033
lotusofsiamlv.com
Mon.-Fri., 11 a.m.-2:30 p.m.;
5:30-10 p.m., daily
$25-$75

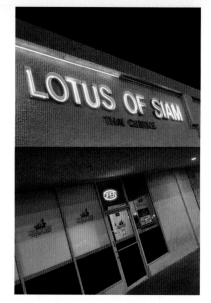

CURTAS

Yogi Berra once said: "That place is so crowded, no one goes there anymore." Truer words were never spoken about LOS.

Ever since Bill and Saipin Chutima took over this space in 1999, it seems every gourmet in the world has beaten a path to their door. So popular has it become with the fiery-foods crowd that a table is almost impossible to score on a weekend evening—when you'll see taxi after taxi dropping off parties large and small every few minutes as tourists make their pilgrimage here to sample our most famous off-the-Strip eatery.

In no other Thai restaurant in town can you find the variety, freshness, and vivid flavors put forth by this kitchen on a daily basis. (Those who had judged Lotus by its lunch buffet were missing the point of this restaurant. Thankfully, they finally discontinued their tepid ode to the all-you-can-eat-crowd a couple of years ago. These days, if you show up for lunch, which also can be crowded if you don't arrive before noon, you get the same menu as the one served at dinner.) The point of Lotus is and always has been the northern and Issan specialties (all in English on the menu), done the way Saipin's mother taught her and well enough to garner her two James Beard Award nominations and (finally), in 2011, the award for Best Chef Southwest (shared with Claude Le Tohic of Joël Robuchon). Pair these dishes with the extraordinary Rieslings that make up one of the best German wine lists in the country.

Add it all up and you have an experience that earns the distinction of being called the best Thai food in the U.S. by Jonathon Gold of the *Los Angeles Times*. Unlike Mr. Gold, I haven't been to every Thai restaurant in the country, but I do tend to agree with him on that score, especially when lingering over bites of Issan sour sausage, koi soi (raw beef with chiles), or Chutima's definitive northern Thai curries. Warning: Gringos should avoid asking for anything "Bangkok hot."

GET THIS: Issan sour sausage; kang hung lay (just because we like saying it); miam kham; khao soi (curry noodles); drunken noodle prawns; catfish larb; nam kao tod (crunchy rice with raw cured pork and peanuts); Panang braised beef; all curries; northern Thai sausage; mango with sticky rice; anything off the northern Thai or Issan menus; any white German or Austrian wine on the phenomenal list, the prices of which are a flat-out steal.

WILBURN

Though the prices and wait time reflect it, Lotus of Siam is completely worthy of the heaping praise it's received. You simply don't know a good tom kha gai until you get one of their hotpots, spice levels cranked up to eleven. Even between the wait, the prices, the painful morning after, and the scariest parking lot in Vegas, it's a restaurant any Thai-lover could go back to any time, any day.

MARCHE BACCHUS (WEST)   French

see map 2, page 251
2620 Regatta Drive Suite 106
(702) 804-8008
marchebacchus.com
Sun.-Tues., 4-8:30 p.m.; Wed.-Thurs., 4-9 p.m.; Fri.-Sat., 4-9:30 p.m.;
Brunch: Sat., 11 a.m.-3:30 p.m.; Sun., 10 a.m.-3:30 p.m.
$25-$75

THILMONT

I always tell people vacationing in Las Vegas and limited to the Strip to visit Spago. But if they have the means to venture into the 'burbs, it's two evocative words: Marché Bacchus.

Located on a bank of the artificial lakes of Desert Shores and not too easy to find the first time, the setting of Marché looks nothing like the Mojave. At the front is a compact wine store where a nice, though not voluminous, selection of vintages is available for take-out or imbibing at dinner or lunch. Beyond is a small dining room.

The real money spot at Marché Bacchus is its waterside patio area. There, under swaying palm trees and flitting hummingbirds, loyal eaters sit down for a largely Gallic menu.

Starter classiques include a faithful French onion soup with Gruyère cheese and a salad of Romaine lettuce hearts Caesar-style. Nicely prepared selections of artisanal cheeses and meats are popular. For a flavorful Parisian experience, the escargot persillade with garlic herb butter is a must.

The menu veers between France and Italy with selections of pasta and risotto. Commendable choices include braised beef ravioli with oyster mushrooms and black-truffle cream; lasagna with duck ragu; and wild-mushroom risotto enriched with mascarpone. Notable entrées include Dover sole with red quinoa, black currants, and pineapple beurre blanc; roasted Wolfe Ranch quail stuffed with foie gras; and seared scallops with broccolini.

I actually prefer Marché Bacchus' lunch service. The lobster-salad croissant is one of my favorite sandwiches in town, or anywhere, really. The authentic buckwheat crêpe with roasted chicken and wild mushrooms in a thyme-infused cream sauce is straight out of a seaside bistro in Brittany. Believe it or not for such a Frenchy place, the burger is worthy—chalk it up to caramelized onions, blue cheese, and roasted tomatoes for toppings.

Expect a long wait for the Sunday brunch when the weather is nice. I go for eggs Benedict with blue crab and asparagus.

For desserts, crème brûlée reigns supreme in the Nevada sun (or nighttime skies).

Again, the scenery around Marché Bacchus makes this restaurant a real experience. I guarantee someone in your party will say, "This doesn't feel like Vegas at all." And it's true every time.

GET THIS: Buckwheat crêpe with chicken and mushrooms; lobster salad croissant; steak frites; duck lasagna; glasses of wine.

CURTAS

Like many a local oenophile, I treat MB like a private club, strolling in and grabbing a bottle from the wine store whenever the urge to drink top-drawer juice at easy-to-swallow prices strikes. There's no beating the burgundies or the slender mark-ups, and owners Rhonda and Jeff Wyatt are always there with a smile and advice when you're looking for something new and interesting to drink. If this place didn't exist in Las Vegas, I'm not sure I would either.

MICHAEL MINA (STRIP) Seafood

Bellagio
(702) 693-8865
bellagio.com
Mon.-Sat., 5:30-10 p.m.
$75-$125

CURTAS

I like to call Michael Mina the Egyptian Wolfgang Puck, and he fits the bill for several reasons. First and foremost is his ability to pull off multiple concepts at all price points, while never losing his street cred as one of the most talented chefs in the business. Secondly, while he's serving up everything from sushi (at Pabu in San Francisco) and football fans at 49ers' games to textbook-perfect French classics (e.g., Bardot Brasserie), he never loses sight of the seafood that made him famous. And finally, like Puck, Mina always makes sure his number-one brand is always in top form. With Puck, that would be Spago and with Mina, it's his eponymous restaurants in San Fran and Bellagio. After long runs in both cities, neither seems to miss a beat, and if you stroll into our MM, you'll find it remains as chic and timeless as a Chanel dress.

The Tony Chi design has aged remarkably well and to these eyes is as elegant as ever, remaining one of the most flattering and comfortable rooms in the business. Just as good is Mina's cuisine: a bit

Eating Las Vegas

less seafood-centric than a decade ago, but just as carefully wrought and beautifully presented.

Start with the tableside-mixed tuna tartare (everyone does), then throw caution (and your cardiologist's advice) to the wind and order the whole lobe of foie gras. Yep, a whole foie, both lobes, roasted to a "T" and carved tableside to the oohs and aahs and envy of everyone else in the dining room. It's as decadent a way to enjoy dinner as there is, but hey, you're in Vegas!

Once you're done hardening your arteries and pissing off the PETA crowd, kick back with a lobster pot pie, still a show stopper after 17 years. Mina never met a piece of pisces he didn't know how to improve upon, and the balance he brings to his sauces and side dishes is extraordinary. P.S. The steaks and lamb are pretty damn good, too.

GET THIS: Tuna tartare; whole foie gras; lobster pot pie, wild king salmon; seasonal tasting menu.

WILBURN

The best part about Michael Mina is his attitude toward his team. He sets his concept and signature dishes, then finds himself a trustworthy exec to marshal the menu. Whoever's at the helm, after 17 years, this eponymous restaurant is still a show-stopper.

Caesars Palace
(702) 731-7888
caesarspalace.com
Sun.-Thurs., 5-10 p.m.; Fri.-Sat., 5-10:30 p.m.
$75-$125

CURTAS

Mr Chow (the man) has been servicing the jet-set glitterati for 40 years, serving them upscale versions of "Beijing cuisine," eaten with forks and knives, in turgid white-tablecloth surroundings that insulate them from the messy realities of real Chinese food and the unwashed masses who might enjoy it. At this, the man is a genius. MR CHOW the restaurant is a place food critics have always loved to hate. That is, until now. Because this fussy connoisseur considers it (along with Carbone, its spiritual Italian cousin) to be a perfect match with Sin City. So perfect, in fact, that we wonder why it took so long for them to get here. This being Vegas, of course, the exclusivity and velvet rope-thing must take a back seat to filling the seats. But fill them they do, in one of our most dramatic dining rooms—a setting that fits this town like a man-bun on a Mongolian.

The circular dining room gives everyone a view of the show—who's coming and going and ordering the $225 Peking duck. The whiteness of the space provides flattering lighting for you and the food, and the size and thickness of the linens tell you you're in for an upscale Asian experience like you (and Las Vegas) have never seen before. The food (that critics from London to Los Angeles have trashed) is about as authentic as a fortune cookie, but none the worse for it. What Michael Chow aims for is elegant versions of both peasant and Mandarin dishes from the Chinese repertoire. Thus will you find superb dim sum, serious squab in lettuce cups, and minced-beef pancakes that are as far from your neighborhood sweet-and-sour palace as Caesars is from Motel 6. Certain hors d'oeuvres , like the chicken curry and turnip puffs, aren't worth the $15 tariff, but most of the menu makes sense if you come with a crowd and share.

What everyone will want to share is the dressed Dungeness crab, a snow white pillow of egg whites holding big chunks of sweet crab, and the oddly named With Three, a stir fry of calves liver, big prawns, and chicken that somehow works. Couples (and those not wanting to spring for the whole bird) will enjoy the smaller portion of Gamblers Duck that's just as crispy, if not as finely tuned, as the show stopper. Both the fluorescent green prawns and the steamed Dover sole will make you sit up and take notice as well.

Purists may balk, but MR CHOW is about unabashed big-deal meal service, a luminous setting, and a sense you're being fed by, and dining with, grownups. It's a throwback in all the right ways, and just the ticket if you value feeling pampered at a price.

GET THIS: Green prawns; squab with lettuce; minced beef pancake; shrimp dumplings; lobster shumai; Mr Chow noodles, with three; Dover sole; Gamblers duck; Peking duck; dressed Dungeness crab; crispy beef.

WILBURN

Hardly another place on the Strip is so simultaneously no-frills and extravagant. If you can get past the giant floating model of an aortic valve in the middle of the dining room, you can enjoy the finest lamb shank with cumin this side of Xinjiang.

OTHER MAMA (WEST)

Raw-Bar

see map 2, page 251
3655 South Durango Suite 6
(702) 463-8382
othermamalv.com
5-11 p.m., daily
$25-$75

CURTAS

Location counts, except when it doesn't. Other Mama may be harder to find than a celebrity chef in the kitchen, but that hasn't stopped every galloping gastronome around from zeroing in on this hidden gem, tucked into an invisible corner in a generic strip mall on south Durango. In a matter of weeks after it opened, Dan Krohmer's ode to great seafood went from "Where's/what's that?" to a "Let's go" on the lips of every foodie in town. These days, it's practically a hangout for off-duty chefs and F&B professionals, as well as the go-to joint for locals seeking serious shellfish.

Nothing about its obscure locale suggests that you're in for top-flight oysters, Penn Cove mussels, or sashimi-grade scallops when you find it. Nor does the name give you a clue—it sounds like a blues bar, and the retro-louche signage suggests a down-on-its-heels absinthe joint you might find in New Orleans. Even when you walk in, things are bit confusing. It's modestly appointed (Krohmer did the build-out himself) with seating for around 50, and the far wall is dominated by a long L-shaped cocktail bar that looks directly into an open kitchen. That bar may look simple, but it's also significant, with mixologist David English shaking, stirring, and conjuring cocktails to a fare-thee-well.

Then you notice a large menu board and things start falling in place. Because Other Mama is an American/Japanese izakaya/sushi/raw bar/gastropub, got that? Krohmer cut his seafood teeth with Iron Chef Morimoto (in Philadelphia) and honed his skills locally at Sen of Japan, just down the street. He specializes in strong flavors paired with impeccably chosen seafood, such as his oysters foie Rockefeller—a dish that combines sweet and salty bivalves with an umami-bomb of duck liver. Everything from the raw bar—from amberjack crudo with Meyer lemon and scallop carpaccio to a sashimi salad with thyme and honey—competes with anything you'll find 10 miles to the east, at two-thirds the price, and his pork-belly kimchee fried rice, seafood toban yaki, and caviar French toast prove Krohmer can pull together proteins and starches in unlikely combinations as well.

Gone are the days when all-you-can-eat sushi bars defined our fish eating off the Strip. Almost overnight, Other Mama upped everyone's game and put to rest the idea that you have to travel to Las Vegas Boulevard South to get the good stuff.

GET THIS: Oysters foie Rockefeller; amberjack crudo; pork-belly kimchee fried rice; Penn Cove mussels.

THILMONT

Over the past year, Other Mama has become perhaps my favorite restaurant in Las Vegas. The unique take on seafood—sashimi meets Latin flair and downhome Southern grub—is approachable, but never simplistic. Even in a city where strip malls rule off-Strip, this is a pretty remarkable find in the western 'burbs. The mixology menu is adventurous and spiritedly delicious, and the happy-hour oysters are a great deal by the dozen.

PICASSO (STRIP) French/Spanish

Bellagio
(702) 693-7223
bellagio.com
Wed.-Mon., 5:30-9:30 p.m.
$125 and up

THILMONT

Nestled gorgeously at Bellagio overlooking the fountains, Picasso is helmed by the much-lauded Julian Serrano, who runs a tight ship in a beautiful room adorned by works of the namesake Spanish master modernist, Mr. Pablo himself.

The absolute star of dining at Picasso is the prix-fixe menu.

The first course offers a selection of crème of parsnip soup with peekytoe crab cake; poached oysters garnished with Osetra caviar and sauce vermouth; and warm quail salad with sautéed artichokes and pine nuts. The quail is one of the dishes people rave about long after they've headed home.

The second course brings a choice of foie gras au torchon with toasted brioche, wild huckleberries, and port wine coulis; sautéed ruby-red Gulf Coast shrimp with roasted zucchini, crispy artichoke, and tomato confit; and sautéed filet of Chilean sea bass with cauliflower mousseline and saffron sauce.

For the decadent third course, choose Maine lobster with sauce

Américaine and salsify; filet of Scottish salmon with mashed celery root and oxtail jus; milk-fed veal chop with rosemary potatoes and jus; pigeon with wild-rice risotto; or medallions of fallow deer with caramelized green apple and Zinfandel sauce.

The "dégustation" menu has highlights such as Alaskan king crab salad with apple-champagne vinaigrette; pan-seared U-10 Day Boat scallop with potato mousseline and jus de veau; sautéed steak of foie gras with crabapple sous vide; and roasted lamb loin with mint aioli and zucchini blossom.

The array of desserts is mind-spinning, including Sauternes-poached pear with almond frangipane, blood-orange butter sauce, and French butter-pear sorbet; warm chocolate fondant with milk-chocolate-orange ice cream and Grand Marnier; and pineapple tart with rum, prickly pear fruit sorbet, and lemongrass granita.

Other esteemed menus include a seasonal truffle roster and a light pre-show selection. Of further note, Picasso has one of Vegas' finest wine programs. Its sommelier-curated flights are essential.

If you're in Vegas for business or romance, a dinner at Picasso is one of the classiest places in town to seal any kind of deal.

GET THIS: Warm quail salad with sautéed artichokes and pine nuts; foie gras au torchon with toasted brioche; wild huckleberries and port wine coulis; sautéed medallions of fallow deer with caramelized green apple and Zinfandel sauce; and Sauternes-poached pear with almond frangipane.

CURTAS

Our most accomplished local chef now has three restaurants to his name, and if I had my way, one of them—Julian Serrano (his tapas restaurant in the Aria)—would be in our top 50. As it is, Picasso has a permanent place in this book as long as his well-nigh-perfect cuisine remains in place. The wine list (and Master Sommelier Robert Smith) should've won a James Beard award years ago, but given that organization's notorious anti-Vegas bias, I wouldn't hold my breath.

PORTOFINO (STRIP)

Italian

Mirage
(866) 339-4566
mirage.com
Thurs.-Mon., 5-10 p.m.
$75-$125

CURTAS

The problem with Portofino is that it serves remarkable Italian food to conventioneers, fanny packers, and bachelorettes who haven't a clue how good it is. Another issue is its location, tucked deep in a corner of a hotel that has seen better days. Portofino is so good and so ignored, one wonders how chef Michael LaPlaca can get up in the morning. As it is, he trudges to work at a collective kitchen he shares with four other restaurants (!) that are, in and of themselves, testament to the middle-brow mediocrity that is the Mirage. Why the Mirage chooses to hide its best restaurant in the farthest corner of the hotel is beyond the capacity of my feeble brain, but the smart money knows to just keep walking past the rest of them until you're practically out of patience, and breath, then look for the overhead sign and a hostess stand. You'll see the actual restaurant once you walk past the bar, where tables suddenly appear and feeding finally becomes an option.

And what feeding it is: hand-cut pastas, melt-in-your mouth gnocchi, and wild-boar Bolognese straight from an Emilia-Romagna nonnina's house. This is the real deal in Italian food, crafted with love and care by a chef who stays true to his roots, while giving everything just the right American twist. Those noodles are the thing to get, and whatever LaPlaca is whipping up in-season is worth the time and trouble it takes to get to it.

This is one of the few restaurants that lavishes as much attention on its big proteins as it does on its appetizers, and the chicken rollatini Parmesan (a creative take on chicken parm) deserves to be enshrined in the Italian-American Hall of Fame.

We're not sure anyone but diehard foodies really appreciate this cuisine, but we're sure happy LaPlaca gets out of bed to make it. The service is as top-notch as the food and the wine list is that rarity of rarities on the Strip: small, carefully chosen, and free of sticker shock.

GET THIS: Grilled octopus; all pastas; braised pork shank; chicken rollatini Parmesan; veal osso buco.

WILBURN

Tucked in the back corner of the Mirage, this space has gone by many names and seen many renovations, but it's currently Portofino by Chef Michael LaPlaca, and I believe it might just be gunning for the most interesting Italian restaurant in Vegas. The items are laborious (and their names sometimes pun-driven), but I believe you'd be hard-pressed to find a better osso buco in town. With one of those, a glass of red, and the 46-year service-industry veteran Will behind the counter, you couldn't have a better stereotypical "Vegas" night.

Bellagio
(702) 693-7223
bellagio.com
5-10 p.m., daily
$75-$125

CURTAS

Prime has been around for 17 years and would be considered just another superior Vegas steakhouse if all the other food it serves wasn't so jaw-droppingly great and the décor the most stunning in the steakhouse business. That décor blends blue and brown in all sorts of romance-enhancing, conversation-inducing, meat-friendly ways. It's not only the prettiest steakhouse in which you'll ever enjoy a ribeye, but also the most comfortable. Everything about the place is designed to soothe and satisfy—from the greeting and the patio (score a table by the water if you can) to food that does the Jean-Georges Vongerichten brand proud.

None of this comes cheap, but you won't find better steaks and sauces anywhere in town, complemented by vegetables and sides that would make a perfect meal all by themselves. Ribbons of tuna swimming in a ginger marinade take your breath away, as do the onion soup and any of the artfully composed salads.

As good as these standards are—can a peppercorn-crusted strip steak with Béarnaise sauce get any better?—the Parmesan-crusted chicken is the real sleeper on the menu. It's a dish most fowl: moist, crispy, and full of chicken-ness (nope, it doesn't taste like chicken; it tastes like *chicken*), and it's a dish even Italian chefs should envy for its crust, cheese, and crackle. The wine list, however, is not for the faint of heart or the parsimonious of pocket.

GET THIS: Onion soup; ribbons of tuna; Dungeness crab cake; seared foie gras with sweet-and-sour morels; Caesar salad; baby iceberg lettuce with Maytag blue cheese; Parmesan-crusted chicken; peppercorn-crusted New York strip; dry-aged bone-in ribeye; pan-roasted Dover sole; duck à l'Orange; every single sauce and every single potato dish.

WILBURN

The lushest of the lush, Prime was one of the New York City stars that Steve Wynn brought in when Bellagio opened. In classic Wynn style, there's more gold leaf and priceless masterpieces on the walls than a Rothschild's bathroom, and Chef Jean-Georges Vongerichten has steakhouse fare to match. Like all good steakhouses, the chicken dish is quietly going to be the staff favorite, and the staff here definitely knows what's up.

RM SEAFOOD (STRIP)

Mandalay Place
(702) 632-9300
rmseafood.com
11:30-10 p.m., daily
$75-$125

WILBURN

The eponymous spot of Top Chef Masters runner-up Rick Moonen has always been the place to experience fish at its most interesting. Over the years, RM has held many industry mixers and fundraisers, and especially recently has turned out superstar chefs. From Johnny Church and Gerald Chin to Justin Kaluba, they've all put their mark on the menu, and now Sean Collins, formerly of Radio City Pizza (the high-concept reincarnation, not the original crap corner), heads the team. It's gratifying to see a seriously experienced and creative chef work with a sustainable seafood concept.

The restaurant is geared toward seafood, but doesn't adhere to any specific cuisine. It's a formless kinda Bruce Lee cuisine that pulls from Thai, Italian, French, traditional New England, Japanese, you name it. Even the supplementary sushi menu, truly a "restaurant inside a restaurant," defies the norms and stereotypes. The sushi itself is a separate beast from the fishy fingers of crackerjack sushi chef Beau Solis, who has the same philosophy about using interesting fish, while also having the freedom to experiment as much as possible.

Dishes like their octopus carpaccio with castelvetrano olives, almonds, and lemon oil succeed in showing off the quality of their main ingredient; the sweet, tender, razor-thin octopus slices far surpass most any boring beef versions. The halibut sashimi with yuzu vinaigrette and Sierra Mist-marinated cucumber is another delightful and playful dish, finished with a grating of dehydrated sea cucumber.

There are permanent menu items for "Rick's Sustainable Catch," a partnership with the Monterey Bay Seafood Watch Program, and Chef's Whole Fish Selection. The sister restaurant upstairs, RX Boiler Room, is a bit less refined, but is a worthwhile part of the team nonetheless. Both the upstairs and downstairs have terrific bar programs, secretly some of the best on the Strip.

Not everything here is from the sea, however. The chefs play around just as well with land animals, though they come in the form of Mary's organic chicken, foie gras torchon, and a handful of steaks. The foie especially can be fun, usually paired with a seasonal berry of some kind.

The desserts are standard fare. No question that they're fitting to the rest of the menu, but I always suggest diners try Rick's Tasting Game. It's a grid of 16 cups of different ice cream and sorbets, plus a blank sheet to put down your guesses on the flavors. This is always a ton of fun, and they definitely like to include some curveballs in the ever-changing list (balsamic strawberry and sweet corn, for example). I suppose I'm just a sucker for this kind of thing, but after a meal of unique dishes and great fish, I'd be happy with whatever comes out for dessert.

GET THIS: Halibut sashimi; oyster trio; octopus carpaccio; foie gras torchon; Chef's Whole Fish Selection; Rick's Tasting Game.

THILMONT

Not to get too environmentally strident, but with all the genetic horror stories of fake-fish switcheroos in the media regarding the fish supply in U.S. restaurants, it's a relief that rm Seafood adheres to the highest standards in sourcing. Go for the daily "sustainable-catch" special. For a celebration, the gigantic Kitchen Sink seafood platter is off the hook!

The Rest of the Best

SEN OF JAPAN (WEST)

Japanese

see map 2, page 251
8480 W. Desert Inn Road
(702) 871-7781
senofjapan.com
Sun., 5-11:30 p.m.;
Mon.-Sat., 5 p.m.-1:30 a.m.
$25-$75

CURTAS

Sen of Japan is the ultimate all-purpose Japanese restaurant. It combines pristine fish, inventive sushi and sashimi, and enough gimmickry to keep serious sushi hounds smiling alongside the California-roll crowd. Whatever your pleasure, Hiro Nakano and his sushi chefs are there to provide it through a multi-page menu that never seems to falter.

A simple omakase of Tokyo-style sushi? No problem. It may not be in the same league as Yui and Kabuto a couple of miles away, but those two don't dazzle you with an array of sauces either. This kitchen specializes in cooking up things like a little cilantro-serrano-miso with your sea bass, or fried capers, yuzu, and lemon olive oil with salmon. Those sauces are applied judiciously and never overwhelm the fish. They are what keep a legion of regulars coming through the door every night. Even better, those omakase dinners are gentle on the pocket ($55 and $85) and showcase what these chefs do best: toggle back and forth between the raw and the cooked. Thus will you be just as impressed with your bracingly fresh oysters as with spoon-tender filet mignon dipped in citrus soy. The udon and soba are always spot-on, as is anything they do with those woodsy-smoky matsutake mushrooms, and what Nakano-san does with soft-shell crab is nothing short of magical. The sake list is solid and there's a late-night happy hour until 1:30 a.m. with serious discounts on various fish dishes and sushi rolls.

S of J is one of those spots I pop into about once a year just to see if it's as ship-shape as ever. Sometimes they recognize me and sometimes they don't, but the food never seems to miss a beat and the service is unfailingly informed, sweet-natured, and fast. Kanpai!

GET THIS: Gyoza; ocean-trout carpaccio; dobin-mushi soup; soft-shell crab sushi roll; Japanese pork with mustard soy; specialty sushi; chef's omakase.

THILMONT

This is where young Grasshopper (meaning the average Las Vegas eater) has gone to get a culinary Japanese education for a decade. And it still rules the school.

SPAGO [STRIP]

Forum Shops, Caesars Palace
(702) 369-6300
wolfgangpuck.com
Sun.-Thurs., 11:30 a.m.-10:30 p.m.;
Fri.-Sat., 11:30 a.m.-11 p.m.
$75-$125

CURTAS

In the beginning, there was Spago. And Spago begat Emeril's. And the success of Emeril's begat Bellagio. And by the turn of the century, all of them, along with many others, had put an exclamation point on the greatest restaurant revolution America had ever seen.

But all that begetting began on December 11, 1992, when Wolfgang Puck opened a branch of his seminal West Hollywood eatery and single-handedly made Las Vegas a player on the world's restaurant stage. Puck tells many stories about that opening: how there were almost no customers the first week; how he told his general manager the whole thing was a big mistake; and how, once the National Finals Rodeo came to town, all the cowboys lined up in front of the open kitchen thinking it was a buffet. Soon enough, they learned just how wonderful the grub was being rustled up by that kitchen.

From day one to nearly 24 years later, it's rarely missed a beat. First under David Robins and currently helmed by Mark Andelbradt, the kitchen never fails to dazzle and surprise, a testament to Puck's perfectionism and one of the most solid staffs in the business. That excellence extends to the front of the house, and has since the get-go—have you ever heard anyone say they had bad service at Spago?

Puck's contributions to America's restaurants are legendary. Open kitchens are everywhere these days, but they started with Spago. The lowly pizza was first given a gourmet cachet by Puck, who was also first to incorporate a casual café in front with a more formal and expensive space in the back of the restaurant.

But most of all, what Puck and Spago did, first in Los Angeles and then in the Forum Shops, was make fine dining fun. They brought good cooking out from behind the curtain and showed America how to have a great time with great food. Once Las Vegas got a taste of everything Spago brought to the table, there was no turning back. Food and beverage executives up and down the Strip knew they had to up their game and that's exactly what they did, causing all of us today, and 42 million visitors a year, to eat better as a result. There was always gold in them thar hills to be sure, but Wolfgang Puck was the first to discover it, and in the process, he begat a sea change in the most tasteful way possible.

GET THIS: House smoked salmon pizza; pizza Margherita; Shanghai noodles; tomato basil soup; Chinese chicken salad; bucatini carbonara; fettucine with wild mushrooms; prime beef burger; roast chicken; steak frites; seafood stew; cookies (best in town); dessert.

THILMONT

For all the history and fanfare, what I like about Spago is that it's a perfectly reliable place to recommend to friends and family staying on the Strip. It's flexible, from the pubby front to the deluxe dining room. Sure, change is afoot after the exit of affable Executive Chef Eric Klein, but it's still a sure bet. Plus, the arrival of Spago really did change Las Vegas—and that's not media hype.

STRIPSTEAK (STRIP)

Steakhouse

Mandalay Bay
(702) 632-7200
mandalaybay.com
4-10 p.m., daily
$75-$125

WILBURN

One thing I've always appreciated about celebrity chef Michael Mina is that he doesn't let his ego get in the way of giving his chefs the recognition they deserve. Some big-name chefs farm the whole menu out to their team, hop a private jet to Vegas twice a year, and take credit for coming up with dishes they might not even have tasted. Some go so far as to include gag orders in their lengthy contracts that prevent their chefs from even speaking to the media. Not all of them, of course, but more than you might assume.

You can tell by Michael Mina's social media alone how transparent he is— sharing his executive and sous chefs' personal Instagram posts, gladly boasting about the superb men and women he has on his team, showing off the fantastic experiments they're conducting in his restaurants. He found Josh Smith to share his dream of a perfected French brasserie for Bardot and he recruited a superstar to take the lead at his steakhouse, Stripsteak, Chef Gerald Chin. Chin had been working the line in Vegas for some time, opening Wicked

102

Spoon in the Cosmopolitan right before joining with Stripsteak.

It's still very much Michael Mina's restaurant, but aside from a few of the fun dishes and the decadent butter poaching prior to wood-grilling his steaks, his Vegas team is responsible for this powerhouse of a menu. In the steak department itself is a wider selection of cuts than most other steakhouses, but if you can hack it, I recommend the World Wide Wagyu tasting: Japanese A5 full-bred Wagyu filet mignon, American Wagyu-Angus crossbreed (I call it Wangus!) rib cap (a.k.a. deckle, a.k.a. spinalis dorsi, a.k.a. "butcher's butter"), and New Zealand grass-fed Wangus braised short rib. Consider this your final test in beef!

What has become Stripsteak's signature dish, the Instant Bacon, is Chef Gerald's baby: five-spice braised, almost candied, pork belly, tempura oyster, and green-cabbage slaw, all smoked under glass for a minute or two, culminating in an explosion of flavor that made Mina himself say, "Oh yeah, that's going on the menu." All the dishes are along the same lines, reflecting a myriad of techniques that honed them to a razor point of perfection. In fact, the menu reads like it was mad-libbed, each dish a mystery of how ingredients like popcorn, edamame, and a king-crab hushpuppy could be combined, but Lord! They all go together so well.

The menu changes drastically by the season, with proteins and preparations switching partners more often a square dance. One day the foie could be three ways (seared slice, torchon, and the cured filling of a macaron … yum!) and the next it could be a tropical "foie-colada" with coconut milk and roasted pineapple. No matter what's being served, it's always mind-blowing and genre-defying. Of course, like all Michael Mina restaurants, the happy hour is great, with Stripsteak's 4-5:30 p.m. bar serving things like house-made corn nuts, Korean wings, Thai beef jerky, or a Wagyu burger you can trust to have actual Wagyu in it.

GET THIS: Instant Bacon; foie gras; World Wide Wagyu; Dr. Joe's duck breast; a drink and a snack at happy hour.

THILMONT

The steakhouse restaurant stretches back in time well more than a century. The wood-burning grill turns out steaks on par with any other Las Vegas chop house, so order away with gusto. The happy hour is a great intro to the eatery.

TWIST BY PIERRE GAGNAIRE (STRIP)

French

Mandarin Oriental
at CityCenter
(888) 881-9367
mandarinoriental.com
Tues.-Thurs., 6-10 p.m.;
Fri.-Sat., 6-10:30 p.m.
$75-$125

Like a few other restaurants in our Top 50, Twist isn't for everyone. Like all restaurants in the Pierre Gagnaire oeuvre, it takes a decidedly adventuresome tack toward most of its menu, which consists mainly of riffs on ingredients presented in a blizzard of small plates. If you're looking for portion size or a standard three-course (app-main-dessert) dinner, look elsewhere. But if you're an intrepid epicure, you'll think you've died and gone to heaven. Which pretty much also describes the room, as heavenly and romantic a space (overlooking Aria and the Crystals Mall) as you'll find on the Strip.

Once you're seated, though, the fun really starts. It's impossible to get bored by Gagnaire's food. The menu changes seasonally and very few "standards" are on it, so whatever I rave about—be it shellfish mariniere with champagne herb sauce and black gnocchi or a trio of savory ice creams—might be long gone by the time you show up. Take heart. This former enfant terrible of French cuisine will capture your attention from the first array of amuse bouche through flights of oyster fancy, accented with everything from sardine rillettes and blue curaçao to frozen bananas. How does he think these things up? Who knows, but they invariably work and keep you smiling and guessing throughout the meal.

If you're saddled with a beef 'n' taters dining companion, don't despair. The steaks here are pricey, but meltingly tender and some of the best in town. Does anyone on Earth make better veal tenderloin? Probably not. Ditto the Bordelaise and Béarnaise sauces. An avant-garde restaurant that also serves tremendous beef (and some of the most stunning vegetarian creations on the planet) sounds like an impossible balancing act, but the chefs here pull off this magic nightly with the consistency of stone masons. The wine list is smaller than those at other top-notch frog ponds, but it's also stocked with some off-beat bottles that won't have you reaching for your respirator when you see the prices.

Speaking of prices, the tasting menus are quite the bargains when compared to the competition. Yet another reason why Twist is so close to our heart.

GET THIS: Vegetarian tasting menu; Pierre's salad; oysters; veal tenderloin; ribeye steak; grand dessert Pierre Gagnaire.

WILBURN

Pierre Gagnaire's only foray into the Western Hemisphere is a successful one, and perhaps all that's necessary to draw the attention to Vegas needed for an update in the Michelin guide ... if those Franco-Japanophile poltroons could ever admit fault and lift their ideological ban on the city that invented the AYCE buffet. Many courses come with additional satellite courses, each of which can be as complex and interesting as the central dish.

WING LEI [STRIP]

Wynn Las Vegas
[702] 770-3388
wynnlasvegas.com
5:30-10 p.m., daily
$75-$125

CURTAS

Confucius said a man cannot be too careful about what he eats, but he obviously never came to Wing Lei—a place where you can just close your eyes and point and still be assured of eating the best Chinese food east of Shanghai. Not only is it our most elegant Chinese restaurant, but it's also one of the most elegant restaurants in all of Las Vegas, period.

From the smooth-as-Shantung-silk white-glove service and the best Peking duck in the business to garlic beef tenderloin of uncompromising tenderness, this is cuisine fit for a mandarin, especially those who like a little posh and circumstance with their Sichuan prawns. Lest you be someone who complains about paying premium prices for shrimp and stir-fries, keep in mind that the Chinese invented the whole shared-plates thing a couple of millennia ago—they just called it family-style—and it's the perfect way to keep portion and check sizes down.

And remember: these dishes are made with first-class groceries (unlike many a run-of-the-mill Chinese restaurant). Executive Chef Ming Yu doesn't know how to put out anything but an exquisite plate of food, and his touch with Cantonese and Szechuan spicing is as graceful as the service. I'm not one for superlatives when it comes to steamed fish, but Yu's light touch with everything that swims takes us straight back to Hong Kong. High rollers from Asia (and we get lots of them) demand perfection in their stir-fries, nutty fried rice, and crispy General Tso's chicken, and Yu delivers it in spades. If you're a fan of any classic Chinese dish, from hand-pulled noodles to kung pao chicken, you'll feel like you're tasting these things the way they were meant to be made, not a version you're settling for in some past-its-prime Chinese dive.

There's nothing past its prime about the wine list, which is stocked with the usual big-hitter bottles for big-ego showoffs. The good news is the (relative) bargains to be found therein and the lower-priced nuggets are the ones that go perfectly with this food. Just look for anything German or Alsatian white, or ask the friendly somms for help.

As for desserts, they give lie to our usual advice about sweets in an Asian restaurant: If you want a good dessert in an Asian restaurant, go to a French one. No offense to Confucius, but the dude really could've learned something from diving into some sesame créme brûlée or a kalamansi cheesecake.

GET THIS: Peking duck; General Tso's chicken; steamed fish; garlic beef; seafood hot & sour soup; Alaskan geoduck clam; Dungeness crab (in season); Santa Barbara prawns; wok-tossed scallops; sampan prawns; mu shu pork; napa cabbage with Iberico ham; Yang Chow fried rice; desserts.

THILMONT

Opulent and royal are fitting descriptions of this gold-toned temple of Chinese dining. It's like a living history book of the world's oldest cuisine. With extraordinary offerings like velvet egg wonton soup, chilled abalone, wok-tossed sea cucumber, and table-side-carved Imperial Peking Duck, you'll need a treasure trove to pay for the all-encompassing experience under the auspicious gaze of an aureate lucky-dragon statue.

YONAKA MODERN JAPANESE (WEST)   Japanese

see map 1, page 250
4983 W. Flamingo Road
(702) 685-8358
yonakajapaneserestaurant.com
5-10:30 p.m., daily; Tues.-Sat., 11 a.m.-2 p.m.
$25-$75

WILBURN

A true off-Strip success story, Yonaka was a quick winner. A couple miles from the main drag is where Ramir DeCastro, owner and chef, has enjoyed a particular following of savvy food lovers. Under the auspices of the subtitle Modern Japanese, the food within will mostly have some references to and techniques from Japanese food, but the spirit of shucking off tradition in favor of creating unique dynamic dishes is as alive here as any fine dining spot on the Strip. Hell, some dishes, like the pork, fennel, and apple creation Meat Candy, feel more Alsacian than anything!

The menu doesn't give due credit to the beautiful plates that come over a humble sushi bar. Descriptions such as "Sake Orenji: Scottish salmon, orange supreme, yuzu tobiko, orange oil, maldon" describe a dish composed of fatty salmon sashimi and a piquant duo of orange oil and skinned wedges of orange (to "supreme" an orange, it's cut away from the center like a cake), and just the touch of salt brings together an incredibly pleasing dish. Another item, started as a special but garnering a great enough reception to be seasonally permanent, is the tate ichigo. Translating loosely to "strawberry banquet," it alternates thick slices of raw Hokkaido scallops and fresh strawberry, along with apricot relish and a strawberry dashi. An interesting combo, no doubt, and like most Yonaka dishes, it brings out some unique flavors from the scallop. Chef Ramir is nuts about seasonal; strawberries start to be paired with plenty when they're in season, from Wagyu to white chocolate.

Despite the impeccable plating and imaginative pairings, Yonaka is deceivingly cheap. Part of their success is definitely the value, as dishes that would be a good $45 if served with Julian Serrano's name attached to it are coming out at $16. Things get even madder at happy hour, with some exclusive items being perhaps their most addictive, like the Hana wings. Much like Thai street wings, these fish-sauce-cured sticky-sweet nuggets of joy are available only between 5 and 6:30 p.m. or 10:30 p.m. to midnight (though they might fry up some if you ask nicely). Their lunch service is similarly a steal, comprised mostly of more relaxed versions of dinner.

Desserts fully cast off any semblance of Asian cuisine and fully embrace modernist haute composition. Honestly, something like their Chocolate Ten Ways would be at home in a place like Sage or Le Cirque without a second thought.

The beauty of Yonaka is that they bring this fine-dining experience at a budget, every single day of the week.

GET THIS: Sake orenji; crispy Brussels sprouts; crudo; Meat Candy; foie gras nigiri; Chocolate Ten Ways; fresh baked cookies and cereal milk.

CURTAS

The first place I send people when they ask me for an interesting restaurant off the Strip. The small-plate and raw-fish concoctions they dream up here are divine and the décor is a nice respite from the hubbub of the hotels.

JOHN CURTAS' BOTTOM 10

Do you enjoy overpriced tourist traps? Tired food? Dated decor? Giving hard-earned dollars to celebrity chefs who are phoning it in? Then Las Vegas has you covered too! Not only does Sin City boast dozens of the world's greatest restaurants, it also hosts more than a few half-baked concepts, licensing deals with "name" chefs, and sad old warhorses, all of which exist solely to separate the gullible from their cash. Proceed to any of these at your own risk, and don't say I didn't warn you.

10. Hush Puppy

Inexplicably popular food that's been served for an unbelievably long time at unexplainably low prices.

9. Hot & Juicy Crawfish

Bags of cheap, nasty, farm-raised, butter-drenched, cayenne-soaked seafood literally dumped (from plastic bags) on slack-jawed hordes who don't mind where their food comes from or how it tastes.

Eating Las Vegas

8. Bob Taylor's Ranch House

Famed mobster Tony "The Ant" Spilotro ate here and the food tastes like it was cooked for his last supper in 1986.

7. Golden Steer Steakhouse

They haven't changed the menu or the carpet here since 1958.

6. Pamplemousse Le Restaurant

Strictly for culinary anthropologists who want to know why French food had a bad reputation in the 1970s.

5. Rivea

Atmospheric space (64 floors above Mandalay Bay) featuring metronomic Italian (by Alain Ducasse, a Frenchman) at stratospheric prices. The food doesn't match the view (to put it mildly) and once you get the bill, you'll want to guillotine someone from both countries.

4. Nobu

Nobu Matsuhisa is cashing in … and you're paying for it.

3. Heritage Steak

Remember when Tom Colicchio was a celebrity chef? Neither do I.

2. Gordon Ramsay Pub & Grill

This place was great for about five minutes when it first opened and El Gordo himself was strolling around kissing babies and shaking hands. Now I wouldn't eat here with Guy Fieri's palate.

1. Olives

In this prime location at Bellagio, you could serve the worst celebrity chef food in Vegas and still make a fortune … and that's exactly what Todd English has done.

John Curtas' Bottom 10

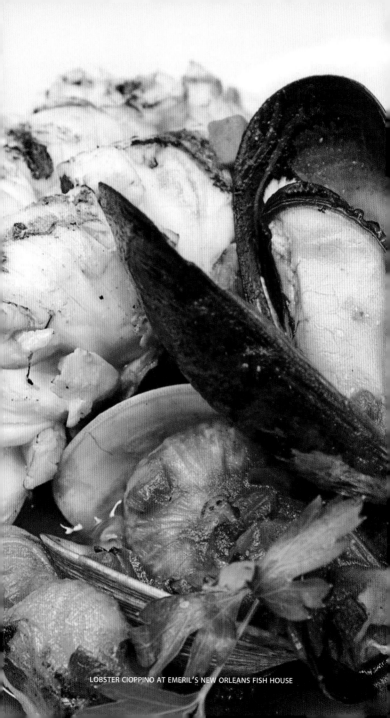
LOBSTER CIOPPINO AT EMERIL'S NEW ORLEANS FISH HOUSE

Section III

Additional Recommendations

CHERRY PEPPER RIBS AT CARBONE

Additional Recommendations
Introduction

Welcome to the third section of our book! By now, you've devoured the Top 10, then forked through the Other 40. After a sweet dessert wine or other postprandial relaxation of your choice, we invite you to forage through the following pages, a wide-reaching look at Sin City's glittering (and sometimes tarnished) culinary landscape. This handy, go-to, finger-on-a-list resource complements the more in-depth reviews and opinions featured so far and includes maps and a place-name index.

This isn't a compendium of every eatery in this neon metropolis. That would be impossible, and not even remotely interesting. Rather, highlighted here is the choice cut, as it were, of this city's overarching menu.

If you don't find a personal favorite listed in this section, especially if it's in the Tourist Corridor, don't be surprised. Many well-known places didn't make the cut. Some are so popular that no matter what they serve, they don't need us to promote them. Others are so ridiculously over-hyped or are such quagmires of feedbag slop that we won' even whisper, let alone type, their rip-off names. And this is a physical book, not a website database. It's so old-school, there's not even an app! And that's the way we like it.

That said, we do have a new section covering a few of the megalithic or noteworthy chain restaurants that seem to make tourists and locals alike go bonkers.

Closer to our mutual hearts, though, is our expanded coverage of various interesting new trends and longstanding Las Vegas areas of culinary expertise. Our brave captain, John Curtas, provides insight

REUBEN-ISH AT GOODWICH

as Vegas' leading dining chronicler of our surprisingly immense Chinatown and all its sundry foodways. Of course, he also wields his formidable chops on steakhouses. Plus, he's added a finely paired section on top wine programs to match the meaty sizzle.

Curtas also names those restaurants he deems deserving of a dressing down for letting diners down in myriad ways. Oh yes, there will be gnashing of teeth and great lamentations over his Bottom Ten critique. There is the root word "tooth" in toothsome, after all.

Our main man with a stylistic drinking plan, Mitchell Wilburn, has likewise focused his literary eye on the Vegas boozy culture with artistic distinction and a chaser of rye.

Yours truly, Greg Thilmont, chipped in with enhanced on-the-street reportage on beer and coffee cultures, as well as additional healthy eating establishments. I've also widened our horizon on Vintage Vegas nooks.

Finally, we called on Anthony Curtis, long-time publisher of the Las Vegas Advisor (and this book), who also maintains the LasVegas Advisor.com website that covers the Las Vegas dining scene extensively; Anthony graciously added his expertise in a few categories, including Late-Night Dining, Special Diet, Local Favorites, and Buffets.

One quick word about locations. Each of the entries in this section includes an address and phone number. When a recommendation has two or three locations, we note that, and when it has more than three, we list as "multiple locations." The address and phone for each are presented according to the following protocol. If there's an original or clearly dominant location, that's the one that's listed. And if not, we list the location that's geographically closest to the Strip. When a restaurant appears in more than one section, the location and phone are provided in the first listing only and subsequent listings refer back.

Cheers! We hope our book proves valuable and thank you for reading.

VEGAN ASSORTMENT AT VEGGIE HOUSE

FOOD

CHINATOWN

When Chinatown Plaza opened in 1995—housing five restaurants and a smattering of shops—Spring Mountain Road was known mainly for its potholes. No one thought of this area as Chinatown and it was audacious of the developers to call it such. Twenty-one years later, all you can do is applaud their prescience and marvel at what this three-mile stretch of road has become.

As of last count, more than 100 Asian restaurants line this avenue (and, it seems, triple that number of massage parlors and nail salons). These days, the whole stretch of street from Valley View to Jones is a veritable buffet of Asian eats and it's a must-stop on any foodie tour of Las Vegas. Intrepid gastronauts know this is where you come to get the real deal in Chinese barbecue, Japanese noodles, and giant bowls of whatever soup suits your fancy—all at criminally cheap prices. For example, dinner for two at Zen Japanese Curry costs roughly what a glass of wine will run you at Wynn/Encore.

Sushi hounds also know that the fish you'll find at Kabuto and Yui is every bit the equal of what you get in the hotels, again at significantly lower prices, and nothing on the Strip competes with the plethora of Japanese izakaya and robatayaki parlors that have popped up in recent years, many open late and catering to the hung over and the about-to-be.

All told, Las Vegas' Chinatown is a treasure in its own right, and the first thing I point to whenever some food snob from New York or San Francisco (they're always from New York or San Francisco) pooh-poohs our food culture as being an inorganic top-down product of too much casino money and too little taste. So grab your chopsticks and dive in.

Some notes about the following list. For the most part, these are places I highly recommend, although a few are noted not for endorsement, but because they're popular and pretty terrible, so I thought you should be forewarned. Almost every restaurant has been visited by me multiple times (I estimate that I've eaten in 98 of the 107 restaurants along Spring Mountain Road). Nevertheless, chefs and owners change sometimes without notice (you'll never see an "Under New Management" sign in an Asian restaurant), so occasionally, dropoffs in cooking quality (e.g., China Mama) occur with no warning.

Finally, none of these joints are for picky eaters. The whole point of eating along Spring Mountain Road is that it's the closest you'll ever get to the real thing without a 14-hour flight across the Pacific. In some of these places, English is definitely a second language. In others, service is, how you say, not of the most professional and friendly quality. But arrive with an open mind and adventuresome palate and you'll be an Asian maven in no time.

Chinese

168 Market
3459 S. Jones Boulevard
(702) 363-5168

Full-service Asian grocery store, probably the best one of the bunch in Chinatown, with fresh fish and takeout galore.

Asian BBQ & Noodle
3400 S. Jones Boulevard #5C
(702) 202-3636

Go well before noon or mid-afternoon if you want to get a seat. Max Jacobson endorsed this as the best Chinese barbecue in Vegas and I have no reason to argue with him. Closed Fridays. (Yes, Fridays. Oh, those crazy Asians.)

CRISPY LION FISH (TILAPIA) FROM CHENGDU TASTE

BBQ King
5650 Spring Mountain Road
(702) 364-8688

Cash only. Cantonese only.

Big Wong
5040 Spring Mountain Road #6
(702) 368-6808

Beef noodle soups to beat the band.

Café Noodle & Chinese Barbecue
4355 Spring Mountain Road #104
(702) 220-3399

Another old reliable that still delivers the goods.

HOUSE SPECIAL SHRIMP FROM CAPITAL SEAFOOD RESTAURANT

Capital Seafood Restaurant
4215 Spring Mountain Road
(702) 227-3588

In the original Chinatown Plaza, going strong for 20 years. Superb Cantonese lobster stir-fries at half the cost you'd pay a mile to the east.

Additional Recommendations

Chengdu Taste
(Essential 50: see page 44)

China Mama
3420 S. Jones Boulevard
(702) 873-1977

Still reliable, but the cooking quality has diminished over time and it's not the force it once was.

Chubby Cattle
3400 S. Jones Boulevard
(702) 868-8808

SPICY DUMPLINGS FROM CHENGDU TASTE

Conveyor-belt hot pot is the mode at this new Mongolian eatery. Some of it is hokey, but the extensive menu has legitimate—and sometimes esoteric—Asian surprises in store.

Crab Childe Yunnan Tasty Garden
5115 Spring Mountain Road
(702) 826-4888

The real deal. No one speaks English; you're surrounded by fellow travelers of all stripes, and (if you're a round-eye) they look at you like you're nuts when you walk through the door. (Expect a lot of "you no like" when you try to order.) Not for the timid, but really really good.

Dumpling King
5740 W. Spring Mountain Road
(702) 257-1486

No pork—it's owned by Chinese Muslims—but that doesn't prevent the xiao long bao (soup dumplings) from being beautiful.

Harbor Palace Seafood
4275 Spring Mountain Road
(702) 253-1688

Another long-standing place that's a big hit with the tour-bus crowd. Haven't been in years, but with so many great newer places, I see no reason to return.

J&J Szechuan Cuisine
5700 Spring Mountain Road
(702) 876-5983

Our favorite, old-school, go-to Szechuan now has serious competition, but still shines.

Joyful House
4601 Spring Mountain Road
(702) 889-8881

One of those truly terrible places that's been around forever. Strictly for the sweet-and-sour-pork crowd.

Niu-Gu Noodle House
3400 S. Jones Boulevard
#16
(702) 570-6363

Those who remember the now-defunct Three Villages will love these dense, addictive, Chinese noodle soups. Limited menu, spotty service, but you won't be able to stop slurping.

Ping Pang Pong
(Gold Coast Casino)
(702) 367-7111

THE TEA CORNER AT NIU-GU NOODLE HOUSE

It's not really in Chinatown.
But it serves some of the best dim sum in town. Unfortunately, you have to brave the environs of the Gold Coast to get to it, and go early: By noon any day of the week, the place is full of Asians and Caucasians fighting for a table.

Sam Woo BBQ
4215 Spring Mountain Road B101
(702) 368-7628

About every other year, this joint gets closed down for a day or two for health-code violations. "So what?" I say. "And when the sun comes up in the morning, does it catch you unawares?"

Additional Recommendations

Szechuan Express
4300 Spring Mountain Road
(702) 685-9600

Another newcomer. Tough to find—tucked in the back of a strip mall near Arville Street—but worth the effort.

BEEF BRISKET WITH TOMATO NOODLE SOUP FROM THE NOODLE MAN

The Noodle Man
6870 S. Rainbow Boulevard
(702) 823-3333

Hand-pulled ribbons are thrown and cut out in the open (they make a show out of it). Noodle Man is a southwest Vegas favorite for its delicious soups and other noodle-based dishes.

Veggie House
5115 Spring Mountain Road
(702) 431-5802

A full menu of classic Chinese dishes and some not-so-classic house specials (try the crispy spicy eggplant), all using vegetarian ingredients only. Open for lunch and dinner, dine-in or take out.

Wendy's Noodle Café
3401 S. Jones Boulevard
(702) 889-3288

Sort of an all-purpose Taiwanese café with pleasant service and an easy-to-navigate menu. A good place to get your feet wet if you're new to this food.

Yi Mei Champion Taiwan Deli
3435 S. Jones Boulevard
(702) 222-3435

Gorgeous soups and Taiwanese street food. Nobody does it better.

Japanese

Hachi Japanese Yakitori Izakaya
3410 S. Jones Boulevard
(702) 227-9300

Another newcomer to our izakaya revolution, Hachi is brand-spanking new, well-run, and more inventive than most.

Ichiza
4355 Spring Mountain Road #205
(702) 367-3151

A grimy second-floor joint that's seen better days, but the food is pretty nifty.

RED SNAPPER CARPACCIO FROM ICHIZA

Izakaya Go
3775 Spring Mountain Road
(702) 247-1183

Sake houses have been popping up like cherry blossoms in April lately, and this is one of the best. The menu is huge, the fish impeccable, and the robatayaki remarkable.

Japanese Curry Zen
5020 Spring Mountain Road #1
(702) 985-1192

If price to value were the only criterion, Zen would beat out Guy Savoy and Joël Robuchon for the best in town. Good gyoza, great spinach curry, insanely cheap prices.

Kabuto Edomae Sushi (Essential 50: see page 76)

Monta Ramen
5030 Spring Mountain Road
(702) 367-4600

Still the gold standard for authentic ramen in Vegas, this extremely popular nook pretty much started Chinatown on its upswing. The dashi (or broth) is supple and sublime. Get there early, as it packs in a crowd regularly, even though it's no longer the only noodle shogun in town.

MISO RAMEN FROM MONTA RAMEN

Eating Las Vegas

Ohjah Japanese Steakhouse
2051 N. Rainbow Boulevard #102
(702) 361-8888

Some Las Vegans might think this local mini-empire (five locations) is just a Benihana-on-the-cheap hibachi-grill knockoff. But especially at the Rainbow restaurant, you'll find surprisingly high-level sushi and beyond. Venture there.

Raku/Sweets Raku (Essential 50: see page 22)

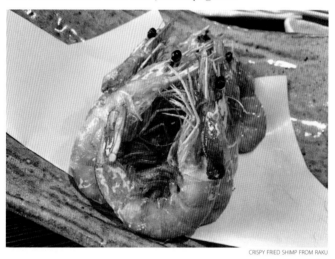

CRISPY FRIED SHIMP FROM RAKU

Ramen KoBo
7040 S. Durango Drive
(702) 489-7788

The owners of perennial-favorite Monta are making their own noodles in this suburban location. The excellent dashi-filled bowls are much spicier here than at the mother restaurant. Konichi-yowza!

Ramen Misoya Tomi
4300 Spring Mountain Road
(702) 998-9781

Not in the same league as Monta and Ramen Sora, but a good alternative when those are packed.

Additional Recommendations

Ramen Sora
4490 Spring Mountain Road
(702) 685-1011

Sapporo ramen—rich, nutty, and sweet—is perfect for a cold day in the desert. Monta's broth may be more refined, but Ramen Sora fills the bill any season (but summer).

Ramen Tatsu
3400 S. Jones Boulevard
(702) 629-7777

Another ramen joint that will do in a pinch when the two superstars, Monta and Ramen Sora, are full.

Sushi Roku (The Forum Shops at Caesars)
(702) 733-7373

A long-time establishment in the tourist corridor that became a bit overlooked has retooled its admirable menu to the adventurous side of sushi while retaining staples like bento boxes. Worth a visit.

Trattoria Nakamura-Ya
5040 W. Spring Mountain Road #5
(702) 251-0022

Wafuu pasta, a Japanese take on Italian food, is the specialty here and dish after dish is fascinating and fun. Order off the big chalkboard and expect some of the most interesting food in town.

Yu Yu Kushiage
4115 Spring Mountain Road
(702) 220-4223

Delicately deep-fried is the specialty, but the sushi and rice dishes are no slouches either.

Yui Edomae Sushi (Essential 50: see page 26)

Korean

Fukuburger
3743 S. Las Vegas Boulevard
(702) 262-6995

Not technically a Korean restaurant, but they put kimchee on some of their (very good) burgers, and that's good enough for me.

Hobak Korean BBQ
5808 Spring Mountain Road #101
(702) 257-1526

Korean 'cue took a big leap forward in the past year and this cacophonous casual spot led the way with better beef and upgraded banchan. If only they'd turn the music down.

MIXED GRILL FROM HONEY PIG

Honey Pig (2 locations)
4725 Spring Mountain Road K / 9550 S. Eastern Avenue #100
(702) 876-8308 / (702) 979-9718

Panchan cooking at its finest. Which means you do all the work on an inverted wok, holding everything from all of those obscure cuts of Korean beef to the last squid standing. Come with a crowd and you'll enjoy yourself. Come as a deuce and you'll wonder what hit you.

Additional Recommendations

Lee's Korean BBQ
6820 Spring Mountain Road
(702) 388-0488

Mr. Lee (owner of a local chain of liquor stores more known for quantity than quality) owns this joint as well and highly recommends it! Or at least that's what the billboards all around town say. Personally, as soon as we see an "all-you-can-eat" sign, we turn the car around.

Magal BBQ
4240 Spring Mountain Road
(702) 476-8833

Of all our new, higher-toned, franchise Korean BBQ joints, this one has the most Seoul. (Sorry.)

Mother's Korean Grill
4215 Spring Mountain Road #107
(702) 579-4745

My go-to spot for dolsot bibimbap and other Korean standards. Not spectacular, but friendly and consistent, unlike some other Korean joints that seem to change ownership more often than I do my socks.

Tofu Hut
3920 Spring Mountain Road
(702) 257-0072

Good cheap bowls of Korean soups that all taste alike to me.

SPICEY CHICKEN FROM MOTHER'S KOREAN GRILL

Thai

Chada Street (Essential 50: see page 42)

Chada Thai & Wine
3400 S. Jones Boulevard
(702) 641-1345

The big brother to Chada Street is smaller and more focused on small plates of traditional Thai food. Either one will have you re-thinking your ideas about this cuisine. As with the offshoot, the wine list is fascinating and fairly priced.

NUA NOM TOK FROM CHADA THAI & WINE

Krung Siam Thai
3755 Spring Mountain Road #102
(702) 735-9485

Old-fashioned Thai. Great lunch special.

Kung Fu Thai & Chinese Restaurant
3505 S. Valley View Boulevard
(702) 247-4120

The granddaddy of Thai restaurants in town. It still does that over-sweet-thing that American Thai restaurants can't get away from, but it's a solid choice, and the yen ta foe (pink noodle soup) is pretty darn scrumptious.

Additional Recommendations

Weera Thai

3839 W. Sahara Avenue #9
(702) 873-8749

It's not technically in Chinatown, which is a couple of miles north, but Weera rates a major wave for its northern Thai specialties, regional variety—Laos and Issan are represented—and beautifully crafted duck dishes.

Vietnamese

We consider Vietnamese food to be something of a cruel joke. No matter how much I try to discern the differences in this or that pho (or the menus, for that matter), I never can. So, rather than strain my brain trying to distinguish these places, all I can do is vouch for them. All of these are good, if remarkably similar. District One is great.

District One (Essential 50: see page 52)

Jenni Pho (2 locations)
4480 Spring Mountain Road / 7855 S. Rainbow Boulevard
(702) 462-9888 / (702) 269-0348

Pho 87
3620 S. Jones Boulevard
(702) 233-8787

Pho Bosa
3355 Spring Mountain Road
(702) 418-1931

Pho D'licious
4631 Spring Mountain Rd #102
(702) 802-3884

Pho Kim Long
4029 Spring Mountain Road
(702) 220-3613

Pho Saigon #8
5650 Spring Mountain Road
(702) 248-6663

PHO TAI FROM PHO 8

Pho Sing Sing
3409 S. Jones Boulevard
(702) 380-2999

Pho So 1
4745 Spring Mountain Road
(702) 252-3934

Additional Recommendations

Pho Vietnam
4215 Spring Mountain Road B201
(702) 227-8618

Viet Noodle Bar
5288 Spring Mountain Road #106
(702) 750-9898

<u>Other Chinatown</u>

Fiesta Filipina
3310 S. Jones Boulevard
(702) 252-0664

Try as I might, I've never enjoyed a single bite of food in a Filipino restaurant. Much like Greek, home cooking is where you'll find the best of this country's cuisine. But if you insist, knock yourself out. The lumpia are less greasy than usual here, but the fish is as over-cooked as ever.

Halal Guys
3755 Spring Mountain Road #101
(702) 848-6162

Get in line with the cheap-eats crowd and expect to be under-whelmed by what gets slopped onto your plate.

COMBO PLATTER FROM HALAL GUYS

Hawaiian Style Poke
3524 Wynn Road
(702) 202-0729

All poke, all the time. Mixed daily. Usually half-a-dozen selections.

Island Malaysian Cuisine
5115 Spring Mountain Road
(702) 898-3388

This restaurant replaced another identical Malaysian restaurant that replaced an earlier restaurant that was indistinguishable from this one. And that pretty much tells you all you need to know about Malaysian restaurants in Las Vegas.

HOKKIEN CHAR MEE FROM ISLAND MALAYSIAN CUISINE

Pokeman
3735 Spring Mountain Road #206
(702) 550-6466

If bowls of rice and a boatload of sushi burritos float your boat, have at it.

Additional Recommendations

Chinatown Desserts

With French, Italian, Mexican, Mediterranean, even American desserts available everywhere, why mess around with Asian? But if you must, all of these do that shaved-ice boba-tea thing Asian teenagers are so crazy about.

Kung Fu Tea
5030 Spring Mountain Road
(702) 776-7077

CRUNCHY COOKIE SNOW FROM SNOWFLAKE SHAVERY

Snowflake Shavery
5020 Spring Mountain Road
(702) 333-2803

Tea Station
4355 Spring Mountain Road
(702) 889-9989

Volcano Tea House
4215 Spring Mountain Road 106B
(702) 207-7414

Crown Bakery
4355 Spring Mountain Road #207
(702) 873-9805

Korean bakeries are a mystery to me. They love to make all sorts of French-sounding stuff puffed up into white-bread cakey concoctions almost identical in texture to one another. Plus, they do that bean paste thing that's almost indefensible. (The Japanese and Chinese are guilty of this dessert misdemeanor as well.) That said, I always enjoy going to the Crown for some coffee and a pastry. Go figure.

Ronald's Donuts
4600 Spring Mountain Road
(702) 873-1032

A family-owned Las Vegas donut institution. The top two shelves are 100% vegan (actually approved by PETA).

APPLE FRITTER FROM RONALD'S DONUTS

Additional Recommendations

SLICED STEAK AT CARNEVINO

HIGH STEAKS:
THE BEST BEEF IN VEGAS

CURTAS

How do you judge a steakhouse?

Is it the quality of the beef? How well they age it? Cook it? The variety of the side dishes? Or is it all about the wine list to you? Or the décor—dark, masculine and clubby, or light, bright, and more modern? Maybe you demand tenderness at all costs? (For the record: a big mistake, since a superior, intensely mineral-rich, roasted-to-exquisite-beefiness strip sirloin should have a fair amount of chew to it.)

Maybe you're service obsessive. Many people are. For them, the warmth of the welcome and speediness of the staff keep them coming back. Perhaps you're a sucker for big bones. Or the type that occasionally gets a hankering for a (less expensive) hanger steak. Or someone who prefers cuts served in less traditional ways. Or likes a lot of folderol with their cholesterol.

Whoever you are, it's a fair bet that you're a conspicuous carnivore and nothing gets your juices flowing like tucking into a haunch of well-marbled steer muscle. If that sounds up your alley, you might consider moving to Las Vegas. Because next to the Big Apple, no city on Earth has better steakhouses than Sin City. And on any given night, I'll put our chef-driven joints up against anything New York City can throw at us.

True, for sheer volume, historical precedent, and breadth of menu options, nothing beats what you find in NYC, but if you look at many Big Apple classics, you'll find a number that haven't changed a thing on their menu in decades. If you close your eyes when you walk into Peter Luger, Keen's, Spark's, Wolfgang's, Gallagher's, Palm Too, and others, then gaze only at your plate, you won't be able to tell whether you're in 1978, 1997, or 2015. Yes, the steaks are magnificent and there's no replacing the testosterone-charged atmosphere in any of them, but in many ways, you're eating in a museum.

Not so in 2017 Las Vegas, where the massive meat emporia give the chefs a lot of latitude to play with their food. These days, seasonal sides are all the rage, and chefs like Matthew Hurley (CUT), Robert Moore (Prime), Sean Griffin (Jean-Georges), Ronnie Rainwater (Delmonico), Nicole Brisson (Carnevino), David Walzog (SW), and David Thomas (Bazaar Meat) make things interesting from season to season, with a plethora of veggies, seafood, and other succulents that can keep even the fussiest gastronome unbored and happy.

Not only that, but between Carnevino's aging program and Bazaar Meat's over-the-top Spanish flair (not to mention that every top house in Vegas now features mind-blowing dry-aged steaks and multiple A-4 and A-5 cuts from Japan), we leave previously preeminent beef bastions like Chicago, Dallas, and Miami running in third, fourth, and fifth places. And if you do that eye-closing plate-gazing thing again, you can't tell the difference between the best of our beef and anything you bite into in midtown Manhattan.

None of these great steaks come cheap. Expect to pay $60+ for a pristine piece of prime, but face it, folks: We all eat too much cow now, so splitting one of these well-trimmed beauties (among two to four people) is the way to go.

No matter what your criteria, you can be assured that your steak might be the best you've ever had and that everything from the taters and foie gras to the desserts will have you dropping your fork in appreciation.

The Top 10 Steakhouses
Andiron Steak & Sea (Essential 50: see page 32)

RIBEYE AT ANDIRON STEAK & SEA

Bazaar Meat (Essential 50: see page 10)

Carnevino (Essential 50: see page 14)

CUT (Essential 50: see page 48)

RIBEYE AT DELMONICO STEAKHOUSE

Delmonico Steakhouse (Essential 50: see page 50)

Gordon Ramsay Steak (Paris Las Vegas)
(702) 946-4663

Every restaurant in Vegas would be a steakhouse if it could be, and Ramsay, one of the best classical chefs in the business, was smart to recognize that fact. This, and his excellent burger joint at Planet Hollywood, keep him waist deep in pounds sterling, but be forewarned, not all Gordon Ramsay restaurants in Vegas are created equal. Mr. Profanity lent his name, but none of his talent, to the Gordon Ramsay Pub & Grill in Caesars. Stick with his steakhouse and burger palace if you want to retain a modicum of respect for what he once was (see "Bottom 10" page 110).

Prime (Essential 50: see page 94)

Strip House (Planet Hollywood)
(702) 737-5200

Sexy décor, sexy drinks, and sexy steaks. 'Tis a pity no locals ever come here, but it's understandable: The location is in a corner of the Planet Hollywood Hotel-Casino so inconvenient that it takes a map and a Sherpa guide to find it. As it is, it's a big hit with middle managers and soccer moms thrilled to be seeing Britney Spears, few of whom has a clue about the great food they're getting.

FILET AT STRIPSTEAK

Stripsteak
(Essential 50: see page 102)

SW Steakhouse
(Wynn Las Vegas)
(702) 770-3325

Since its makeover last year, this Wynncore money machine looks less like a bus station and more like a Brobdingnagian beef emporium. The bar was slightly enlarged and the lighting softened, but there's still no disguising that the fact that you're in a 300-plus-seat meat market. For that reason, get a table on the patio. Correction: Insist on a table on the patio. That way you'll feel cozy and cosseted, and ready to be charmed by all sorts of David Walzog riffs on classic steakhouse dishes. The wine list isn't priced for those in need of a pacemaker.

DOUBLE-CUT RIBEYE AT SW STEAKHOUSE

Honorable Mention

N9NE Steakhouse (if you can stand the noise level), **Circus Circus Steakhouse** (if you can stand the hotel), **Lawry's The Prime Rib** (an old standby that still delivers), **Charlie Palmer Steak** (a recent upgrade has got this place humming again), **Jean-Georges Steakhouse** (beautiful food, lousy décor), **Hank's Fine Steaks** (if you can stand driving to Henderson), **Tender** (great game in season, if you can stand the Luxor), **Japaneiro** (a few miles west of the Strip, for an Asian take on great steaks).

NEW YORK STRIP AT JEAN-GEORGES STEAKHOUSE

Bargain Steaks

Las Vegas is famous for its bargain steak and prime rib dinners, many of which run off and on as promotions in the casinos. The following are ongoing best bets for finding a good steak for under $20: **Ellis Island, Herbs & Rye, Hitchin' Post Saloon and Steakhouse, Irene's, Jacksons Bar & Grill**, and **Rincon de Buenos Aires**.

FILET-CUT SIRLION STEAK SPECIAL AT ELLIS ISLAND

Additional Recommendations

STEAK FRITES AT BARDOT BRASSERIE

FRENCH

Las Vegas is blessed with more great French food than anywhere in America that isn't New York City. The food our French chefs turn out every day, be it in a restaurant, brasserie, or bistro, tastes like you're a stone's throw from the Champs-Élysées. We had our own little French Revolution here (2005-2010), which saw names like Robuchon, Boulud, Gagnaire, and Savoy plant their flags on these desert shores, and their standards of excellence continue to be the bar by which all chefs measure themselves.

Bardot Brasserie (Essential 50: see page 8)

Bouchon (Essential 50: see page 38)

Delices Gourmands French Bakery
3620 W. Sahara Avenue
(702) 331-2526

A couple of miles west of the Strip in a strip mall that's seen better days, you'll find one of our better bakeries. Not much on décor, but the breads are très fantastique and the crêpes, huge baguette sandwiches, and canelés de Bordeaux are the genuine articles.

EATT Healthy Food
7865 W. Sahara Avenue #104
(702) 608-5233

Three young French fellows are trying to show a Las Vegas neighborhood that real French food can be as healthy as it is delicious. And they do. And it is.

Eiffel Tower Restaurant (Paris Las Vegas)
(702) 948-6937

They probably do more weddings here than in all other Vegas restaurants combined. Solid (if unimaginative) French fare amidst one of the most dramatic settings at which you will ever swoon over a soufflé.

Additional Recommendations

Guy Savoy (Essential 50: see page 64)

SEA BASS WITH DELICATE SPICES AT GUY SAVOY

Joël Robuchon (Essential 50: see page 74)

L'Atelier de Joël Robuchon (Essential 50: see page 18)

Le Cirque (Essential 50: see page 20)

Marché Bacchus (Essential 50: see page 82)

Mon Ami Gabi (Paris Las Vegas)
(702) 944-4224

Best people watching in town (on the patio); best three-meals-a day French restaurant in town.

Patisserie Manon
751 W. Charleston Boulevard #110
(702) 586-2666

Popular west-side neighborhood spot on the cusp of Summerlin. It doesn't hold a candle to Rosallie or Bouchon, but its macaroons and quiches will do in a pinch.

FRENCH ONION SOUR AT PATISSERIE MANON

Payard Patisserie and Bistro (Caesars Palace)
(702) 731-7292

Incredible pastries and chocolates, though the bistro fare is not what it once was.

Picasso (Essential 50: see page 90)

Rosallie Le French Café
6090 S. Rainbow Boulevard
(702) 998-4121

Awesome pastries. Superb quiches. Serious coffee. The only thing I don't like about Rosallie is how far it is from my house.

Twist by Pierre Gagnaire (Essential 50: see page 104)

ROYAL OSSETRA CAVIAR AT TWIST

Additional Recommendations

THE BUFFET AT WYNN LAS VEGAS

BUFFETS

Bacchanal Buffet (Caesars Palace)
(702) 731-7928

Quality was their mission and you can say they've out performed every other buffet on that measure. Where else can you get Gordon Ramsay's fish-n-chips and Nobu's black cod on the same plate?

The Buffet (Aria)
(702) 590-8630

A buffet with a tandoori oven! Load up on skewers here, plus hit the mozzarella bar and charcuterie station, both worth the price of admission by themselves.

The Buffet (Bellagio)
(702) 693-8111

Bellagio has never slacked in its quest for pomp and the buffet has kept up the tradition. The weekend brunch goes above and beyond, with its unlimited lobster and caviar, and what other Vegas buffet has a chef's tasting table? Answer: None.

PLATED CAVIAR OFFERINGS AT BELLAGIO BUFFET

Additional Recommendations

The Buffet (Wynn Las Vegas)
(702) 770-3340

Steve Wynn tried to outdo himself and this may be the one spot where he did truly improve over Bellagio. Even things like quail and king crab legs (none of that snow-crab garbage) fill the steam trays, and of course tons of dim sum, Steve's own food fetish.

Cravings (The Mirage)
(702) 791-7111

A big selection includes noodle soups and salads made to order, and dim sum for breakfast. Cravings is less expensive than others of its ilk and the best play is lunch, which is similar to dinner, only for several dollars less. Note that take-out service is also available (unusual).

Feast Buffet (Station Casinos)
(702) 558-7000

Station Casinos' Feast buffets are hands-down winners on a price-to-quality comparison, plus all meals are discounted with the casinos' players card.

Wicked Spoon (Cosmopolitan)
(702) 698-7870

Like the Cosmopolitan itself, the buffet here opted to be as unorthodox as possible, while still being enjoyable. Probably the best brunch buffet in this price range, if for the slab-bacon carving station alone. As with Cravings, take-out service is also offered here (guess that's not so unusual anymore).

WICKED SPOON BUFFET AT THE COSMOPOLITAN OF LAS VEGAS

Eating Las Vegas

BURGERS

Bachi Burger (multiple locations)
bachiburger.com

Unusual, innovative, and now at both ends of town.

SPICY MISO BURGER AT BACHI BURGER

B&B Burger & Beer (Venetian/Grand Canal Shoppes)
(702) 414-2220

Mario Batali does burgers! And his tribute to the In-N-Out dou-ble-double is fantastic.

Bobby's Burger Palace (The Shops at Crystals)
(702) 598-0191

Bobby Flay's burgers trump anything he's doing at Mesa Grill, al-though the burger there is also one of Vegas's best.

Burger Bar (Mandalay Place)
(702) 632-9364

Hubert Keller was the first fancy chef to bring a burger concept to Las Vegas and his are still some of the best.

Carnevino (Essential 50: see page 14)

Awesome meat. Awesome burger.

Carson Kitchen (Essential 50: see page 40)

Kerry Simon's butter burger is a legacy that does his memory proud.

CUT (Essential 50: see page 48)

Get the sliders at the bar.

Delmonico Steakhouse (Essential 50: see page 50)

Unlike most steakhouses (Carnevino being the exception), it's open for lunch and the burger is the thing to get with a nice glass of vin rouge.

Fatburger (multiple locations)
6775 W. Flamingo Road
(702) 889-9009

Next to Smashburger, this is my favorite franchised meat patty on a bun.

Fat Choy Restaurant (Eureka Casino)
(702) 794-0829

Sheridan Su's fusion burger is a piled-high delight.

Five Guys
7580 S. Las Vegas Boulevard #120
(702) 431-0055

I like Five Guys. I like Smashburger better, but I like FG enough to put them in this book.

Fleur by Hubert Keller (Mandalay Place)
(702) 632-9400

When a fine French chef does a bison burger like this one, we pay attention.

Fukuburger (see page 129)

They put everything but the kitchen sink on these pan-Pacific patties, and if that's your thing, have at it.

Glutton (Essential 50: see page 62)

Bradley Manchester's Glutton Burger will go toe to toe with anything a celebrity chef throws at you. The house-made cheese sauce alone makes it worth a special trip.

FAT CHOY BURGER

Gordon Ramsay BurGR (Planet Hollywood)
(702) 785-5462

This is actually our favorite of the bombastic Brit's four Vegas eateries. And shhhhhh … don't tell anyone, but the hot dogs are just as good as the burgers.

HELL'S KITCHEN BURGER AT GORDON RAMSAY BURGER

Holsteins Shakes and Buns (Cosmopolitan)
(702) 698-7940

Perfect for when your nightclub buzz is wearing off at The Cosmo.

In-N-Out Burger (multiple locations)
4888 Dean Martin Drive
(702) 768-1000

Classics never go out of style. Nor does this "secret menu." Do you get yours "animal style"?

Marché Bacchus (Essential 50: see page 82)

A serious burger in a stunning setting.

N9NE Steakhouse (Palms)
(702) 933-9900

We prefer a burger at the bar to a steak in the ear-splitting dining room.

Shake Shack (2 locations)
New York-New York / Downtown Summerlin
(725) 222-6730 / (702) 964-1025

Danny Meyer took this concept public to great acclaim … on Wall Street no less. Aficionados know his is but a tepid ode to In-N-Out, at a substantially higher price. Still, people line up for them, so who are we to argue?

Smashburger (multiple locations)
Caesars Palace
smashburger.com

See Five Guys, page 152.

Steak & Shake
9777 S. Las Vegas Boulevard
(702) 933-0880

I've been eating Steak & Shake burgers since I was six. These new franchises try to re-capture the glory of smashed grilled burgers, skinny fries, and Chili Macs from the '60s, but lack the proper seasoning that comes with great memories.

Stripburger (Fashion Show Mall)
(702) 737-8747

Decent burgers and shakes; great people watching.

Umami Burger and Beer Garden (SLS Las Vegas)
(702) 761-7614

The burger that Los Angeles made famous is now in one of our best sports bars.

White Castle (Casino Royale)
(702) 227-8531

The original sliders are now on the Strip, muting the munchies and helping to halt hangovers at 4 a.m.

VEGGIE BURGER FROM UMAMI BURGER AND BEER GARDEN

Additional Recommendations

BLOODY MARY SIDECART AT HEARTHSTONE

BRUNCHES

Andiron Steak & Sea (Essential 50: see page 32)

Besides having the fanciest shrimp cocktail on God's green Earth, this is an over-the-top Hamptons-style brunch with a superb lobster roll, serrano ham and eggs, the ever-sinful mac-n-cheese waffle, and the best people-watching in Summerlin.

Bardot Brasserie (Essential 50: see page 8)

Perfect brunch. Wear a tie. End of entry.

Border Grill (Essential 50: see page 36)

A unique brunch featuring unlimited table service from about 20 items. Yucatan eggs Benedict, guava empanada, machaca chilaquiles—mmm!

Bouchon (Essential 50: see page 38)

This was the King of Brunch until Bardot came along, but it's still amazing, making you feel like a trust-fund kiddie or a reality-TV star, and for the price, it had better.

Glutton (Essential 50: see page 62)

Hipsters love brunch almost as much as they love Ira Glass and correcting people. The effort shows: Everything here has as much grace and aplomb as their dinner.

WATERMELON SALAD AT GLUTTON

Hearthstone (Essential 50: see page 70)

Super sidecart for bloody Mary maniacs.

Additional Recommendations

Kitchen Table

1716 W. Horizon Ridge Parkway #100, Henderson
(702) 478-4782

Some fancy stuff for Hendertucky. If you find yourself on the uninteresting side of the Vegas valley, treat yourself to some funky fresh grub and Mexican hot chocolate. Any menu with a section just for foie gras definitely has my undying love.

Marché Bacchus (Essential 50: see page 82)

A beautiful setting overlooking the lake at Desert Shores.

Makers & Finders Urban Coffee Bar

1120 S. Main Street #110
(702) 586-8255

Brunch favorites with a South American twist, plus some really fancy and expensive coffee drinks served by, and to, people you can tell have way too much sex for their own good.

Weiss' Deli

2744 N. Green Valley Parkway, Henderson
(702) 454-0565

Oy vey, this place is more kosher than compounding interest (though not strictly glatt). Nowhere else can you get a whitefish salad, chopped liver, or a mountain of corned beef that even comes close.

CHICKEN NOODLE MATZO BALL SOUP AT WEISS DELI

DESSERTS

ACE Donuts
9435 W. Tropicana Avenue
(702) 222-3370

Family owned and operated and completely fantastic.

RASPBERRY CRONUT AT ACE DONUTS

Allegro (Essential 50: see page 30)

Leave the gun, eat the cannoli!

Art of Flavors
1616 S. Las Vegas Boulevard #130
(702) 457-5522

Former executive pastry chef Doug Taylor has brought this storefront back from the brink with a revamped cozy interior, made-to-order churros, and various lip-smacking, smooth-as-silk, frozen treats.

Additional Recommendations

Carson Kitchen (Essential 50: see page 40)

The desserts change seasonally and never more than a few are on the menu, but your table will be fighting for the last bite.

Chef Flemming's Bake Shop
7 S. Water Street B& C, Henderson
(702) 566-6500

There are precious few reasons ever to venture to downtown Henderson, least of all to eat, but this little shop is a gem and worth the journey.

CRAFTKitchen
10940 S. Eastern Avenue, Henderson
(702) 728-5828

Warm flaky goodness baked from scratch and grandmother-approved.

Delmonico Steakhouse (Essential 50: see page 50)

Steakhouse dessert used to be nothing but cheesecake and peach melba. Not so at Delmonico, where Diane Wong knows how to keep purists and fussy foodies alike satisfied.

Gelato Messina
2010 Festival Plaza Drive #130
(702) 848-1688

A super-cool Australian import in Downtown Summerlin. Get the chocolate fondant, for sure!

Gelatology
7910 S. Rainbow Boulevard #110
(702) 914-9144

Desyree Alberganti's inventive gelatos are worth finding. Spoon-suckingly awesome, it's by

BLUEBERRY YOGURT GELATO AT GELATO MESSINA

far the best gelato in town. (And that includes all the fancy restaurants in all the fancy hotels).

Hexx Kitchen + Bar (Paris Las Vegas)
(702) 331-5100

Carol Garcia does bean-to-bar chocolate on a par with anything you'll find on either coast, and the rest of her sweets and shakes ain't too shabby either.

Lulu's Bread & Breakfast
6720 Sky Point Drive
(702) 437-5858

Big, fat, flaky, fruity pastries on the north side of town, with some interesting fresh-baked breads to take home with you, too.

PINEAPPLE PUFF SUNDAE AT LUV-IT FROZEN CUSTARD

Luv-It Frozen Custard
505 E. Oakey Boulevard
(702) 384-6452

An original slice (or cup, as it were) of Las Vegas' sweet side. A must-do.

Mothership Coffee Roasters
2708 N. Green Valley Parkway, Henderson
(702) 456-1869

Single-origin cold-brewed coffee on tap is complemented by pastries made using whole wheat flour all the way from Washington state.

Additional Recommendations

Rosallie Le French Café (see page 147)

An authentic slice of homey Southern French baking, bringing freshly made high-quality pastries and desserts to the desert.

Rose. Rabbit. Lie. (Cosmopolitan)
(702) 698-7440

Some of Ben Spungin's creations need to be seen to be believed. Chocolate dirt, anyone?

Serendipity 3 (Caesars Palace)
(702) 731-7373

If there's a show on TV about Vegas sweet treats, this fun place's nutso sundaes and ice-cream layer cake are bound to be highlighted.

TREASURE CHEST AT SERENDIPITY 3

Spago (Essential 50: see page 100)

Kamel Guechida oversees the dessert programs at all Wolfgang Puck outlets and, to a venue, they're wonderful.

Suzuya Pastries & Crepes
7225 S. Durango Drive #101
(702) 432-1990

Remarkable pastries in the southwestern part of town.

Eating Las Vegas

Sweets Raku (Essential 50: see page 22)

Twist by Pierre Gagnaire (Essential 50: see page 104)

Vivian Chang creates an array of sweets that dazzle and perplex as only Gagnaire can.

Yardbird Southern Table & Bar (Venetian Hotel-Casino)
(702) 297-6541

Lots of Southern-style fried, baked, and whipped goodness.

PORK CHOP AT B&B RISTORANTE

ITALIAN

THILMONT

Allegro (Essential 50: see page 30)

Located in the often overly opulent Wynn, this is an approachable place for ravioli with dandelion greens and pancetta. Reasonably priced for the venue.

Andiamo Steakhouse (the D)
(702) 388-2220

A luxurious plate of potato gnocchi with Madeira wine-laced wild-mushroom ragu will justify a visit downtown.

Battista's Hole in the Wall
4041 Linq Lane
(702) 732-1424

The complimentary house wine isn't vintage, but it is super-fine in its own way! This is the much-loved Italian restaurant that closed in your hometown years ago.

B&B Ristorante (Essential 50: see page 34)

Do visit for squid ink pasta with 'Njuda sausage or rabbit "porchetta" with Brussels sprouts from Mario Batali and Joe Bastianich.

Bottiglia Ristorante & Enoteca (Green Valley Ranch Resort)
(702) 617-7075

Created by the folks who brought you Hearthstone, this is a bright energetic restaurant that puts a modern touch on Italian cuisine mixed with lots of wood-fired aroma.

Carbone (Essential 50: see page 12)

Waiters in velvet jackets. Veal marsala the size of a hubcap. Settle in! Bring money.

Additional Recommendations

Casa di Amore
2850 E. Tropicana Avenue
(702) 433-4967

Old Vegas east of the Strip. Chow on cioppino and osso buco while being entertained by live Rat Pack-style singers. Plus, free shuttles from the Strip. Dino and Sammy would approve.

Cucina by Wolfgang Puck (The Shops at Crystals)
(702) 238-1000

The Wolf's fancy pies include tomatoey margherita and several cured wood-fired meat-laden combos.

Ferraro's Italian Restaurant & Wine Bar
(Essential 50: see page 60)

Gino Ferraro has one of the best Italian wine lists in the city, and runs that rarest of creatures: a venerable Italian restaurant that's gotten better.

AGNELLO IN CROSTA AT FERRARO'S ITALIAN RESTAURANT

Fiamma (MGM Grand)
(702) 891-7600

Pawan Pinisetti produces passels of pulchritudinous pasta, albeit in a restaurant the size of an airplane hangar.

Eating Las Vegas

Giada (Cromwell)
(855) 442-3271

A bit controversial for its idiosyncratic, glammed-up, and pricey interpretations of pastas and such, but this is a star-powered notable draw nonetheless.

Italian-American Club Restaurant
2333 E. Sahara Avenue
(702) 457-3866

Generations of paisans, and their friends, gather at this supper club to socialize, listen to live music, and dine on escarole & beans and a big selection of "Basta Pastas."

CRAZY ALFREDO AT NORA'S ITALIAN CUISINE

Nora's Italian Cuisine
5780 W. Flamingo Road
(702) 873-8990

A big menu packed with every conceivable variation on pastas, pizzas, and parmigianas. Recently built its own new building with a sparkling bar, patio dining, and a bocce ball court.

Pasta Shop Ristorante & Art Gallery
2525 W. Horizon Ridge Parkway, Henderson
(702) 451-1893

A funky little nook in the southern 'burbs. The house specialty of squid-ink pasta with tiger shrimp and saffron cream sauce is a must do.

Additional Recommendations

Piero's Italian Cuisine
355 Convention Center Drive
(702) 369-2305

An Italian-American restaurant that would make Fellini feel at home. Eat your agnolotti with spinach at the storied "Monkey Bar."

Portofino (Essential 50: see page 92)

The breakout Italian cuisine success of recent Vegas history is Portofino, where innovations like crab-filled arancini and ripatelli with wild boar ragu are stunning.

VEAL OSSO BUCO AT PORTOFINO

Rao's (Caesars Palace)
(702) 731-7267

Sit down for serious dining with Uncle Vincent's lemon chicken, spicy meatballs, and eggplant Parmesan. After dinner, play bocce ball in the heart of the Caesars Palace pool complex.

Salute Trattoria Italiana (Red Rock Resort)
(702) 797-7311

Out in Summerlin, Salute is raising the bar for Italian food with a beautiful room and menu stars like crispy zucchini blossoms, salt-crusted baked branzino, and linguine with vodka sauce flambéed in a hollowed-out wheel of Parmesan cheese.

Eating Las Vegas

MEATBALLS AT RAO'S

Sinatra (Encore)
(702) 770-5320

An elegant tribute to the Chairman of the Board offering up several of Ol' Blue Eyes' favorite dishes.

Italian (Pizza)

THILMONT

Amore Taste of Chicago
3945 S. Durango Drive
(702) 562-9000

The top place in town to get a deep-dish pie and pay big-shouldered tribute to "da Bears."

Additional Recommendations

Dom DeMarco's Pizzeria & Bar
9785 W. Charleston Boulevard
(702) 570-7000

Nestled in tony Summerlin, Dom's brings New York quality to Las Vegas' pizza panorama. President Obama famously ordered dozens of pizzas delivered during an overnight Vegas stay.

CHEESE PIZZA WITH VEGETARIAN SAUCE AT DOM DEMARCO'S PIZZA

Due Forni Pizza & Wine (Essential 50: see page 54)

Wood fires fuel fantastic pies in this local gem far from the Tourist Corridor, including one with truffle cream!

Grimaldi's Pizzeria (multiple locations)
Venetian/Grand Canal Shoppes
(702) 754-3448

Coal-fired brick ovens—straight outta Brooklyn, yo!

Metro Pizza (muliple locations)
4001 S. Decatur Boulevard
(702) 362-7896

Hands down, this is the best general pizza local chain in Las Vegas.

Naked City Pizza Shop (2 locations)
3240 S. Arville Street / 4608 Paradise Road
(702) 243-6277 / (702) 722-2241

They're famous for their Buffalo-bred meatball-mounded "Guinea Pie" and gourmet 'zas.

Pizza Rock (2 locations)
Downtown Grand / Green Valley Ranch
(702) 385-0838 / (702) 616-2996

Home to perhaps the grandest and most expansive array of pizzas in town. Get one of the best slices in Vegas from the counter at the front of the downtown location.

Secret Pizza (Comospolitan)
(702) 698-7860

Up your cool factor by finding this hot, but hidden, slice vendor.

Settebello Pizzeria Napoletana (2 locations)
9350 W. Sahara Ave. #170 / 140 S. Green Valley Parkway, Henderson
(702) 901-4877 / (702) 222-3556

Consistently fine pies in the original style of Naples. Some new-bies are taken aback by burnt thin crusts—the very reason to go there.

FIORE E PESCHE PIZZA AT SETTEBELLO PIZZERIA NAPOLETANA

Additional Recommendations

YUCATAN PORK TACOS AT BORDER GRILL

MEXICAN

Border Grill (Essential 50: see page 36)

China Poblano (Cosmopolitan)
(702) 698-7900

Don't let the China-meets-Mexico vibe fool you: everything from the cochinita (Yucatan-style) barbecue pork tacos to the pozole rojo soup are some of the best versions you will ever taste.

Carlito's Burritos
4300 E. Sunset Road, Henderson
(702) 547-3592

Really more New Mexican than Mexican, but the best place in town for some spicy adovada or a serious sopaipilla.

El Menudazo
3100 E. Lake Mead Boulevard #18, North Las Vegas
(702) 944-9706

Way out of the way, up in the heart of North Las Vegas, where most gringos fear to tread. Our advice: Go for lunch and get a huge bowl of pozole.

El Sombrero Mexican Bistro
807 S. Main Street
(702) 382-9234

Formerly the oldest operating restaurant in Sin City. It's been re-habbed and the menu redone, but it's still in its original location.

Frijoles & Frescas
4811 S. Rainbow Boulevard
(702) 483-5399

Good not great, but the frescas are fun, and the lines are out the door.

Komex Express
633 N. Decatur Boulevard H
(702) 646-1612

Korea-meets-Mexico-fusion-fun, or, put another way: bulgogi meets the burrito. There's nothing subtle about this food, but it's wildly and inexplicably popular with a certain sort of chowhound.

FISH TACOS AT KOMEX EXPRESS

La Comida
100 S. 6th Street
(702) 463-9900

Serious Mexican cuisine and a motherlode of tequilas. A must for lovers of all things agave.

Lindo Michoacan (multiple "Michoacan" locations)
2655 E. Desert Inn Road
(702) 735-6828

Fresh tortillas, amazing margaritas, and lots of lengua (tongue) keep us coming back to the original on East Desert Inn. The off-shoots around town aren't nearly as good.

Los Antojos
2520 S. Eastern Avenue #2
(702) 457-3505

Holy hole-in-the-wall, Batman! This is the only reason ever to venture to East Sahara!

Los Molcajetes
1553 N. Eastern Avenue
(702) 633-7595

Another out of the way place on the Las Vegas/North Las Vegas border, with large volcanic molcajetes (thick, round, stone mortars) holding all sorts of spicy stews. Don't speak English? No problem, since few others in the joint do either. The servers, however, are very sweet and helpful to us gueros.

COCHINITA REVOLCADA AT LINDO MICHOACAN

Mexican (Tacos)

Abuela's Tacos
4225 E. Sahara Avenue
(702) 431-0284

The house-made tortillas alone are worth the trip.

Tacos El Compita
6118 W. Charleston Boulevard
(702) 878-0008

Better than most, not as good as others.

CARNE ASADA TACOS AT TACOS EL COMPITA

Eating Las Vegas

Tacos El Gordo (2 locations)
3049 S. Las Vegas Boulevard / 1724 E. Charleston Boulevard
(702) 982-5420 / (702) 251-8226

An authentic taqueria with the language barrier to prove it. Get in line and point and prepare to be impressed.

Tacos El Rodeo Barbacoa Estilo Hildago
2115 N. Decatur Boulevard
(702) 638-1100

You order at the counter and sit in a no-frills windowless room. You notice three incendiary salsas at a counter, grab a flimsy fork, and wait. Then the tacos show up and you wonder why you don't eat here every day.

Tacos Mexico (multiple locations)
1800 S. Las Vegas Boulevard
(702) 444-2288

For when you really really need a taco at 2 a.m.

Taqueria El Buen Pastor (multiple locations)
301 S. Decatur Boulevard
(702) 432-5515

Guadalajara street tacos to beat the band. Look for the taco wagon at the corner of Bonanza and Las Vegas Boulevard to nab some righteous al pastor beauties, 24/7.

Additional Recommendations

UNI AT YONAKA MODERN JAPANESE

SUSHI

Fish N Bowl
7225 S. Durango Drive
(702) 739-3474

Howard Choi's hole-in-the-wall puts forth some incredible, inventive sushi.

Hiroyoshi Japanese Cuisine (Essential 50: see page 72)

Kabuto Edomae Sushi (Essential 50: see page 76)

SASHIMI ASSORTMENT AT KABUTO

Katsuya by Starck (SLS Las Vegas)
(702) 761-7611

I don't know what's prettier: the room, the fish, or the women who dine here.

Naked Fish Sushi & Grill
3945 S. Durango Drive A6
(702) 228-8856

Westside hang where you're apt to see a television poker pro or two around World Series of Poker time. Check the blackboard for the live shrimp (when it's in season).

Additional Recommendations

Soho Japanese Restaurant
7377 S. Jones Boulevard
(702) 776-7778

Westside sleeper, building a big reputation with sushi aficionados.

Sushi Fever
7985 W. Sahara Avenue #105
(702) 838-2927

For the California-roll lover in you.

Yellowtail Japanese Restaurant & Lounge (Bellagio)
(702) 730-3900

Inventive fish. Fabulous sake list.

Yonaka Modern Japanese (Essential 50: see page 108)

Yui Edomae Sushi (Essential 50: see page 26)

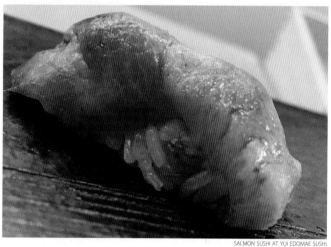

SALMON SUSHI AT YUI EDOMAE SUSHI

Yuzu Japanese Kitchen
1310 E. Silverado Ranch Boulevard
(702) 778-8889

Gorgeous, authentic omakase and kaiseki meals served to a neighborhood that has no idea how great the food is.

All-You-Can-Eat Sushi

Given all the great sushi restaurants in Vegas, the AYCE route doesn't make much sense to me. But I've included these (kicking and screaming) as the best of the bunch for those who's thing it is. (All are $21-$22 for lunch and $26-$27 for dinner.)

Blue Fin Sushi & Roll
3980 E. Sunset Road #102
(702) 898-0090

Small but mighty. One of the best neighborhood AYCE sushi joints.

Goyemon Sushi House
5255 S. Decatur Boulevard #118
(702) 331-0333

We know Japanese natives who will eat AYCE sushi only here.

Jjanga Japanese Restaurant
3650 S. Decatur Boulevard
(702) 453-3377

Not for purists—despite the name, it's Korean-run—but the product is good and this is a fun party place (or at least it can be—

CATERPILLAR ROLL AT GOYEMON SUSHI HOUSE

Jjanga had to reapply for a liquor-license, call ahead).

Oyshi Sushi
7775 S. Rainbow Boulevard
(702) 646-9744

The only AYCE sushi in town that I can truly tolerate. Fresher than most. More inventive than most. More authentic than most.

Sushi Mon (2 locations)
9770 S. Maryland Parkway #3 / 8320 W. Sahara Avenue #180
(702) 617-0241 / (702) 304-0044

Same owners as Goyemon. Nuff said.

Additional Recommendations

SANGRIA ROJA AT HEARTHSTONE

CHEAP EATS/
LOCAL FAVORITES

Alder & Birch (The Orleans Hotel & Casino)
702-365-7111

This steak-centric new eatery in a somewhat old off-Strip casino features handsome modern design reminiscent of something in Seattle or San Francisco. Dine on Wagyu beef or Jidori chicken here quite more affordably than two miles east on Las Vegas Boulevard.

Andiron Steak & Sea (Essential 50: see page 32)

In the summer, this place looks like a Tommy Bahama outlet. Prepare to overhear a guy in pink shorts talking about his complicated workout routine.

Big Wong (see page 121)

It's located in a strip mall with some of our priciest eateries, but everything here—noodle soups, curries, shrimp wontons—is priced below $10. The jalapeño chicken wings are insane!

The Blind Pig
4515 Dean Martin Drive
(702) 430-4444

Though in a rather hard-to-find yet "it's right there!" location in the Panorama Towers west of the Strip, this comfortable brick-lined restaurant melds diner-style grub with good Italian dinner service.

Casa Don Juan
1204 S. Main Street
(702) 384-8070

Getting a seat in this place is nearly impossible on weekends. Nonetheless, it's a rite of passage for southern Nevadans.

Additional Recommendations

CRAFTkitchen

10940 S. Eastern Avenue, Henderson
(702) 728-5828

This darling of the southern stretches of the metropolitan area has a breakfast- and lunch-oriented menu that reflects contemporary tastes. Think red velvet pancakes and avocado toast.

Doña Maria Tamales Restaurant

910 S. Las Vegas Boulevard
(702) 382-6538

A pilgrimage place for Las Vegans of all stripes for corn-husked masa packets.

Echo & Rig

440 S. Rampart Boulevard
(702) 489-3525

Cheap beef (with lots of interesting choices) and no corkage keep it afloat.

BONE MARROW CARNE ASADA AT ECHO & RIG

Fat Choy Restaurant (see page 152)

A casino diner that serves the unexpected—e.g., steamed bao and duck fried rice alongside short-rib grilled cheese and kalbi steak & eggs. Expect to be impressed.

Fat Greek Mediterranean Bistro
4001 S. Decatur Boulevard #34
(702) 222-0666

Family-owned hot spot for lunch, TFG serves authentic Greek/Armenian fare made from scratch. Leave room for the awesome desserts and pastries.

CHICKEN WINGS AT FLOCK & FOWL

Flock & Fowl
380 W. Sahara Avenue
(626) 616-6632

Poached chicken, shmaltz rice, broth, and dips. So simple, but there's a reason why it's one of the most popular dishes in Asia. Good chicken wings, too.

Forte European Tapas Bar & Bistro
4180 S. Rainbow Boulevard
(702) 220-3876

This Bulgarian-Armenian-Hungarian-Greek-Russian-Spanish tapas bar has been a hit with foodies and Vegas' Central European community since day one. Don't miss the flavored vodkas or a chat with owner Nina Manchev.

STUFFED SWEET PEPPERS AT FORTE EUROPEAN TAPAS BAR & BISTRO

Harrie's Bagelmania
855 E. Twain Avenue #120
(702) 369-3322

Bagels, smoked fish, bountiful breakfasts, and big deli sandwiches till closing at 3 p.m.

Home Plate
2460 W. Warm Springs Road
(702) 410-5600

A sports bar that takes its food seriously. Serves up excellent pizzas and one of the best clam chowders in town.

Honey Salt
1031 S. Rampart Boulevard
(702) 445-6100

Soccer-mom food.

John Mull's Roadkill Grille
3730 Thom Boulevard
(702) 645-1200

This butcher shop, on a ranch, in a residential area way up on the north side of town, serves combo plates of barbecued ribs, brisket, hot links, rib tips, tri-tips pork, and chicken, with apple or peach cobbler for dessert.

Kitchen Table (see page 158)

Though somewhat remotely located near the edge of Henderson, this modernistic kitchen attracts eaters from across the valley for upscale huevos rancheros, kale salad, and other shibboleths of New American cuisine. All is prepared and presented in magazine-photo-caliber crockery.

Lola's A Louisiana Kitchen (2 locations)
241 W. Charleston Boulevard / 1220 N. Town Center Drive
(702) 227-5652 / (702) 871-5652

Good gumbo, jambalaya, étouffée, po boys, and killer charbroiled oysters.

Lulu's Bread & Breakfast (see page 161)

In other cities across the Western U.S., eateries like LuLu's are the norm. In Las Vegas, it stands out for all the morning and midday reasons. If you love the great outdoors like I do, it's the perfect stop on the way to hiking at Mt. Charleston or fueling up your human engine before setting out into the desert up Highway 95. Go for the Benecio del Porko and all its hollandaise goodness.

Mary's Hash House
2605 S. Decatur Boulevard #103
(702) 873-9479

Not "a go go"! Corned beef, roast beef, ham, chicken, or combo hash, served with grits and homemade jellies.

M&M Soul Food Café
3923 W. Charleston Boulevard
(702) 453-7685

This nondescript lunch counter puts forth superb fried chicken and waffles, cornbread, collard greens, corned-beef hash, and decent-enough barbecued ribs to make you think you're almost in Mississippi.

SHRIMP CREOLE AT LOLA'S

Nora's Italian Cuisine (see page 167)

This long-operating local fave serves large portions off a big menu with almost nothing priced at more than $20.

Norm's Eggs Café
3655 S. Durango Drive
(702) 431-3447

Possibly the largest breakfast menu in town, from omelets and Benedicts to pancakes and frittatas—even an off-menu creamed chipped beef on toast. Breakfast and lunch only.

Other Mama (Essential 50: see page 88)

OYSTERS FROM OTHER MAMA

Paymon's Mediterranean Café & Lounge (2 locations)
4147 S. Maryland Parkway / 8380 W. Sahara Avenue
(702) 731-6030 / (702) 804-0293

Barely-average Mediterranean fare, but the extended-happy hour prices have made these a favorite among the undiscerning.

Perù Chicken Rotisserie (2 locations)
2055 E. Tropicana / 3886 W. Sahara Avenue
(702) 732-0079 / (702) 982-0073

The rotisserie chicken is good, but the prize here is the ceviche, made with chunks of "premier" sea bass and served with potato, corn, and toasted corn on the side.

Rollin Smoke Barbeque (2 locations)

3185 Highland Drive / 725 S. Las Vegas Boulevard
(702) 836-3621 / (702) 462-9880

Hopping off-the-beaten path lunchtime destination, Rollin' Smoke cooks its 'cue in big outdoor smokers, Razorback countrystyle.

Roma Restaurant & Deli

5755 W. Spring Mountain Road
(702) 871-5577

This bustling Italian restaurant, deli, and bakery is the real deal for lunch or dinner. Try a hot or cold sub on their fresh-baked bread. Warning: The cookies are addictive.

Standard and Pour

11261 S. Eastern Avenue #200, Henderson
(702) 629-5523

The same team behind Carson Kitchen with a more polished Henderson concept. Some truly wild dishes, all of them real winners no matter how crazy they sound.

Tap House

5589 W. Charleston Boulevard
(702) 870-2111

Famed for its pizza and wings (half-price late nights and all weekend). Monday's free open mic sessions pack the back room with aging mobsters and their dolled-up dames—real-life time traveling!

Todd's Unique Dining
4350 E. Sunset Road, Henderson
(702) 259-8633

Todd Clore is at the stoves every night, keeping Henderson well fed and giving us a reason to travel there.

Vila Algarve
6120 W. Tropicana Avenue #11-12
(702) 666-3877

Family-owned and serving authentic Portuguese cuisine, with a splash of Greek and a penchant for seafood.

Vintner Grill
10100 W. Charleston Boulevard #150
(702) 214-5590

Nothing about this place is as good as its reputation.

Zaytoon Market & Restaurant
3655 S. Durango Drive
702-685-1875

Located on the west side (right next to the amazing Other Mama, in fact), Zaytoon boasts some of the best Persian cuisine in town, from kebabs to dried barberry-festooned saffron rice that looks like jewels on your plate. The charred lavash bread is fantastic. Wash it down with an emerald-toned tarragon soda.

BEEF KOOBIDEH AND CHICKEN KABOB FROM ZAYTOON MARKET & RESTAURANT

CLASSIC VEGAS

Battista's Hole in the Wall (see page 165)

Bric-a-brac fills the dining rooms. So do tourists slamming complimentary red wine. It's a fun throwback kind of place, but not a gourmet palace.

BATTISTA'S HOLE IN THE WALL

Bootlegger Italian Bistro
7700 S. Las Vegas Boulevard
(702) 736-4939

Drive to this happening nightspot for a good selection of Italian-style food and plenty of top-notch lounge music, especially jazz.

Chicago Joe's Restaurant
820 S. 4th Street
(702) 382-5637

This downtown Vegas jewel is a tribute to old Italian-American kitsch. The pasta lunch special is a must.

Additional Recommendations

El Sombrero Mexican Bistro (see page 173)

Golden Steer Steakhouse
308 W. Sahara Avenue
(702) 384-4470

A shrine to yesteryear with leather booths and a famous Caesar salad (that doesn't justify its fame anymore). The Rat-Packers all ate here and plaques over selected tables designate where they sat.

Hitchin' Post Saloon and Steakhouse
3650 N. Las Vegas Boulevard
(702) 644-1220

A classic value-steakhouse located on the far north end of Las Vegas Boulevard. Its five steak dinners are all priced under $19. Eat in the little enclosed steakroom, at the bar, or on the outside patio next to a horseshoe pit.

Hugo's Cellar (Four Queens)
(702) 385-4011

This subterranean spot has seen many romantic dinners over the Vegas ages. The tableside salad is a local classic.

HUGO'S CELLAR

192

Eating Las Vegas

Italian-American Club Restaurant (see page 167)

Operating since 1961, the IAC was originally a men's social club boasting a membership that included Frank Sinatra, along with several other showbiz and "sporting" types. Those kinds of guys still come around, but it's mostly for the pasta and live entertainment.

Lawry's The Prime Rib
4043 Howard Hughes Parkway
(702) 893-2223

Though born in L.A. and not a true Vegas original, it's been here long enough to be vibrantly vintage. It does perfect prime rib and Yorkshire pudding in a clubby timeless setting. Popular with the business and convention crowd, at least at the executive level.

Michael's Gourmet Room (South Point)
(702) 796-7111

Old school swankiness at a steep price paid mainly by knaves, rubes, and the nouveau riche.

Mt. Charleston Lodge
5375 Kyle Canyon Road
(702) 872-5408

Though lack of parking and crowds are logistical problems, the trek up to this alpine establishment in a forest far above deserty Las Vegas is mandatory for locals. Enjoy a boozy mug of hot coffee laced with Drambuie and brandy, which should be sipped on the deck.

Omelet House
2160 W. Charleston
(702) 384-6868

The eggy breakfasts and decrepit fern-bar motif are straight out of the tacky '70s, but it's near and dear to many a local's hearts. A booth is reserved for famous former Mayor Oscar Goodman and his wife, Carolyn, the current mayor.

Pamplemousse Le Restaurant
400 E. Sahara Avenue
(702) 733-2066

A Gallic joint named by crooner Bobby Darin that somehow hasn't given up the ghost.

Peppermill Restaurant and Lounge
2985 S. Las Vegas Boulevard
(702) 735-7635

PEPPERMILL FIRE PIT

Visiting the Peppermill at night, basking in its neon glow and getting buzzed, is a de rigueur locals rite of passage.

Piero's Italian Cuisine
[see page 168]

A certain type of middle-manager/car salesman/real-estate huckster-type will tell you Piero's is the greatest Italian restaurant in town. They tend to be the parents of the lounge lizards who think the same thing about Panevino.

Pioneer Saloon
310 NV-161, Goodsprings
(702) 874-9362

A 45-minute drive southwest of Vegas brings you to the unmistakable Pioneer Saloon in the wilds of the Mojave Desert. It's great, especially when there's live music. Try the Ghost BBQ Burger (fired with the magma-like Bhut jolokia pepper) and a cold beevo, or get caveman fancy with a huge tomahawk ribeye steak for two. It's been here since 1913. Bikers and photographers love this place.

The Bagel Café
301 N. Buffalo Drive
(702) 255-3444

Nevada movers and shakers, plus many others, flock here for bialys and a worthy matzo ball soup.

Top of Binion's Steakhouse (Binion's Gambling Hall)
(702) 382-1600

Venture to the 24th floor of the namesake downtown casino to enjoy chicken-fried lobster and a glass of vino with one of the best views in town.

Vickie's Diner
1700 S. Las Vegas Boulevard
(702) 444-4459

Known for decades as White Cross Drugs, this diner is still serving breakfasts, burgers, and more, 24/7.

PEACH SALAD FROM GLUTTON

DOWNTOWN DINING

Bocho Downtown Sushi
124 S. 6th Street
(702) 750-0707

Downtown's only dedicated sushi house is mostly geared for the AYCE and happy hour crowd, and the happy hour is a good one with 30% off your entire bill.

Carson Kitchen (Essential 50: see page 40)

Chow
1020 Fremont Street
(702) 998-0574

This hipster hangout focuses on fried chicken and Asian-style dishes like riblets and pot stickers.

Cornish Pasty Co.
10 E. Charleston Boulevard
(702) 862-4538

A beer-happy corner gathering place in the Arts District with a motherlode of hand pies. Some heartily harken back to mining days with stuffings of ground lamb and rutabaga; others are global, such as chicken tikka and salmon in white wine-dill sauce inside their edible crusts.

Eat
707 Carson Avenue
(702) 534-1515

People line up here for truffled-egg sandwiches and veggie burgers. The workable repast has garnered a somewhat mystifying hype.

El Sombrero Mexican Bistro (see page 173)

Glutton (Essential 50: see page 62)

The Goodwich (Essential 50: see page 66)

La Comida (see page 174)

Le Pho
353 E. Bonneville Avenue #115
(702) 382-0209

From the chef of District One, home of the best pho in town. Deep cuts from Vietnamese street food, mild to wild. Small menu, but literally 100% winners.

PAD THAI FROM LE THAI

Le Thai
523 Fremont Street
(702) 778-0888

Max Jacobsen (one this book's original authors) wrote of Le Thai: "[owner] Daniel Coughlin, who grew up in a Thai family, uses his grandmother's recipe—lots of cilantro, garlic, and fiery spice. It's the best pad thai I've eaten outside Thailand."

PublicUS
1126 Fremont Street
(702) 331-5500

Coffee perfection by some truly obsessives, backed up by very hip small plates and solid baked goods. For the hippest of hip.

Eating Las Vegas

Siegel's 1941 (El Cortez Hotel & Casino)
(702) 385-5200

An informal and fun place to revisit old-school dishes like the Kentucky hot brown sandwich, Midwestern walleye, liver and onions, and more "ordinary" fare.

Smashed Pig Gastropub
509 Fremont Street
(702) 444-7816

Very competent Brit food, certainly better than most other English in Vegas, and a sticky toffee pudding that would make Gordon Ramsay crème his anglaise.

Triple George Grill
201 N. 3rd Street
(702) 384-2761

Only a decade or so old, this place brought non-casino class to downtown when it was totally absent.

VegeNation
616 Carson Avenue #120
(702) 366-8515

Vegan food done right by chefs who know how to cook and season all sorts of plant matter, this is one of the few places in downtown Las Vegas where it's always tough to get a table. And when you get tired of eating the healthy stuff, they have a full liquor license and some tasty cocktails to destroy your liver with.

SAVE THE TUNA FROM VEGENATION

Additional Recommendations

Zydeco Po-Boys
616 E. Carson Avenue #140
(702) 982-1889

Proving that a po-boy doesn't have to be popcorn shrimp in a baguette, there are some fun and funky combinations to try here, definitely a worthwhile spot.

LATE NIGHT

WILBURN

Allegro (Essential 50: see page 30)

Open until 6 a.m., daily.

American Coney Island (the D)
(702) 388-2120

Detroit-style chili dogs and loose hamburger. Open 24 hours, daily.

AMERICAN CONEY ISLAND DOGS

Badger Café
1801 E. Tropicana Avenue # 8
(702) 798-7594

If you've had a rough night, sometimes the only life-saver you can get when the sun is rising is a big ham steak and enough fried potatoes to choke a horse. Open 24 hours, daily.

Bootlegger Italian Bistro (see page 191)

Former showgirl and lieutenant governor Lorraine Hunt's family has owned The Bootlegger since 1949. It's changed locations over the years, but it still relies on the same tried-and-true family recipes. And you never know what Strip performers might stop by late at night to work out some new material on the dining-room stage. Open 24 hours, daily.

Capriotti's
4480 Paradise Road
(702) 736-6166

Las Vegas' only 24-hour Capriotti's is located across the street from the Hard Rock.

Casa di Amore (see page 166)

Open until 5 a.m., daily (closed Tuesdays).

Chada Street (Essential 50: see page 42)

Open until 3 a.m., daily (closed Mondays).

Chada Thai & Wine (see page 131)

Open until 3 a.m., daily (closed Mondays).

El Dorado Cantina
3025 Sammy Davis Jr. Drive
(702) 722-2289

Open 24 hours, daily.

SHRIMP TACOS FROM EL DORADO CANTINA

El Taco Feliz
4755 W. Flamingo Road
(702) 247-6633

Slingin' the best hard-shell tacos in town and part of the loveably divey Money Plays bar (see page 220). Open 24 hours, daily.

Food Express (Palace Station)
(702) 367-2411

Thank the Asian clientele at this off-Strip casino for the menu of authentic Chinese dishes, including rainbow jellyfish and hot and spicy duck feet (for less-adventurous diners, there's always the chicken chow mein). Provides tableside dim sum service to players in Pit 8 (Asian games), too. Open until 3 a.m., daily.

Halal Guys (see page 134)

Open daily until 4 a.m.

Herbs & Rye
3713 W. Sahara Avenue
(702) 982-8036

Open until 4 a.m., daily (closed Sundays).

Honey Pig (see page 129)

Open 24 hours, daily.

Hong Kong Café (Palazzo)
(702) 607-2220

Hong Kong street food hits the Strip, with house specialties that include Macau-style roasted pork belly, fried fish ball with curry, and King seafood Vietnamese noodle soup. Open until 1 a.m. weekdays, 3 a.m. Fri./Sat.

MACAU-STYLE ROASTED PORK BELLY FROM HONG KONG CAFÉ

Hong Kong Garden Seafood & BBQ Café
3407 S. Jones Boulevard
(702) 878-8838

Late-night hot pot. Open 24 hours, daily.

Ichiza (see page 125)

A perennially popular late-night hangout with the student crowd, who show up mainly for the addictive Honey Toast (so simple; so good!) Open until 2:30 a.m., daily.

Krung Siam Thai (see page 131)

Open until 5:30 a.m., daily.

Musashi Japanese Steakhouse
3900 Paradise Road
(702) 735-4744

Sushi, teppanyaki dining, and a late-night happy hour are the big draws at this eatery (request Chef Tiger Woo for top #NSFW entertainment value). Open until 4 a.m., daily.

Noodle Asia (Venetian)
(702) 414-1444

Specializes in large portions of rice, noodle, and congee dishes; vegetarian specialties; and soups. Open until 3 a.m., daily.

Peppermill Restaurant and Lounge (see page 194)

Breakfast, bar snacks, and upscale coffee shop fare. Open 24 hours, daily.

Ping Pang Pong (see page 123)

Open until 3 a.m., daily.

Pin-Up Pizza (Planet Hollywood)
(702) 785-5888

The largest slices on the Boulevard, served by "pin-up"-styled waitresses—perfect late-night munchies! Open Sun.-Thurs., 2 a.m.; Fri.-Sat., 4 a.m.

Raku
(Essential 50; see page 22)

PIN-UP PIZZA

Still a bustling scene after midnight, the small-plates here are the perfect healthy solution for late-night munchies. Open until 2 a.m., daily.

Eating Las Vegas

Soyo Korean Barstaurant
7775 S. Rainbow Boulevard #105
(702) 897-7696

Hip neighborhood hangout, popular with a younger crowd. Authentic Korean cuisine (sometimes with a twist), served small-plate style by a friendly English-speaking staff. Open until 3 a.m. (Fri. & Sat., 4 a.m.; Sun., 2 a.m.).

Vickie's Diner (see page 195)

Classic old-school soda fountain somehow survives within the dilapidated vestiges of the famous former White Cross Drugs. Open 24 hours, daily.

Wolfgang Puck Bar & Grill (MGM Grand)
(702) 891-3000

From 11 p.m. nightly, when good boys and girls have gone to bed, The Wolf breaks out a late-night menu featuring everything from buttermilk pancakes and steak & eggs, to Jidori Half-Chicken and Linguine & Clams. Open until 6 a.m., daily (2:30 a.m. Tuesdays).

THE CHAIN GANG

Chick-fil-A (2 locations)
S. Eastern / St. Rose Parkway, Henderson

All three of this book's authors really do wonder—and don't give a rooster's gizzard about the corporate politics here—why in the h-e-double-hockey-sticks so many Las Vegans have been salivating like Pavlovian poultry since the announcement that this chain was setting up shop here. They're just chicken sandwiches, for Pete's sake!

Cracker Barrel (2 locations)
8350 Dean Martin Drive / 2815 E. Craig Road
(702) 474-1120

The latest cult restaurant to test the Las Vegas market serves southern-style comfort food and elicits "love it" to "just a shrug" rea reactions. But with 650 outlets in 43 states, a whole lot of people are lined up on the love-it side.

Dave & Buster's
2130 Park Centre Drive, Downtown Summerlin
(702) 984-4800

The food is somewhere between gastropub and bar food. Work off the calorie bombs with vigorous matches of skee-ball!

Giordano's (Grand Bazaar Shops at Bally's Las Vegas)
(702) 736-4988

In my estimation, Chicago deep-dish pizza is really more of a casserole than a flatbread, no matter the ingredients that fill it. Nonetheless, this virtuoso of the pile 'o' pie has millions of big-shouldered fans, and now you can dig into one on the Strip.

Eggslut (Cosmopolitan)
(702) 698-7000

Hipster skinny jeans got tighter when this outpost of the L.A. food media darling pitched a tent in the Cosmopolitan. It's pretty tasty, but a tad precious. Its comestibles could definitely be food porn on the cover of Auspicious Apricot magazine, though!

The Habit Burger Grill (multiple locations)
365 Hughes Center Drive
(702) 838-0593

Another California burger company that's invaded the Las Vegas market. Seriously, how many bun-and-patty joints does a city of 2.3 million need? Regardless, it has a good product that's a bit more gourmet than In-N-Out.

In-N-Out Burger (see page 154)

Mmmmm. This is a tasty burger! I think In-N-Out Burger is the true Big Kahuna of fast food in the Southwest, having gotten its start in southern California in 1948 (introducing the first drive-through). Las Vegas' first satellite on Tropicana west of the Strip opened in the late '90s. Go for the "secret menu" if that's your animal-style thing.

Shake Shack (see page 155)

Another NYC-to-Vegas transplant, this place sends some burger lovers into an all-out tizzy. My taste buds on the subject are, well, meh. Decent, but not worth all the fanaticism. Still, both locations draw hordes.

PEOPLE/
CELEBRITY WATCHING

Andiamo Steakhouse (see page 165)

The D's Italian Steakhouse has proven to be a hit with the famous friends of flamboyant casino owner Derek Stevens, including stars of UFC, WWE, and NASCAR and the casts of TV's "Pawn Stars" and "Sons of Anarchy."

BILL GOLDBERG AT ANDIAMO STEAKHOUSE

Bazaar Meat (Essential 50: see page 10)

"This is why you are here!" chef José Andrés—who eats whatever makes him "feel like a lion"—roars from the menu, but there are no human sacrifices of starlets or socialites in the fire pit and this restaurant's vibe is designed to be as playful as the cuisine and its creator.

Border Grill (Essential 50: see page 36)

Patio views of the famous Lazy River at Mandalay Beach, or of the hordes enjoying some high-end retail therapy in the Forum Shops—take your pick from the "Too Hot Tamales" two Vegas locations, both of which offer plenty of people-watching potential from a relaxed, social vantage point.

Eating Las Vegas

CRUSH (MGM Grand)
(702) 891-3222

If you want to catch Rick Moonen nibbling on gnocchi, George Strait savoring a steak, Dita Von Teese dining on a Date & Artichoke Flatbread, or Bruce Buffer toying with Tuna 2 Ways, this place would be your best bet to do it.

CUT (Essential 50: see page 48)

Proprietor Wolfgang Puck knows the whole of Hollywood and many of his famous fans choose to get their steak fix here when slumming in Vegas.

Hexx Kitchen + Bar (see page 161)

JOE JONAS AT CRUSH

The new hangout for sweet-toothed celebs—from rapper 50 Cent to Playmate Kennedy Summers—is also giving neighbor Mon Ami Gabi a run for its money, with its matching patio views of the passing hoi polloi on Las Vegas Boulevard.

La CAVE (Wynn Las Vegas)
(702) 248-3463

Katy Perry, Amber Rose, Troy Aikman, Neil Patrick Harris, Yeardley Smith, Michael McDonald, Patrick Monahan, Sebastian Maniscalco, Kenny Mayne, Nick Cannon, Akon—it would probably be quicker to list the celebrities who haven't yet been spotted at this place …

LAVO Italian Restaurant (Venetian)
(702) 791-1800

This perennially popular "haute" spot has added an extra dimension to its restaurant/nightclub offerings, with the debut of LAVO Casino Club, where grand-opening night saw rapper Busta Rhymes joining celebrity host, actor Joe Manganiello, at the blackjack tables.

KIM KARDASHIAN AT LAVO

Mon Ami Gabi
(see page 146)

With perfect views of the Bellagio Fountains, this French bistro overlooking the Strip remains among our top picks for observing the herd on the street.

MR CHOW (Essential 50: see page 86)

The seventh wonder from Michael Chow is where J. Lo chose to celebrate her opening night at Planet Hollywood, and is also where (show)room-mate Britney Spears' held her big New Year's Day bash.

Old Homestead Steakhouse (Caesars Palace)
(877) 346-4642

From DJ megastar Calvin Harris, to actor Morgan Freeman, you never know who might be dining at this Las Vegas transplant of the historic New York original that claims to be the inventor of the doggy bag.

Rx Boiler Room (Mandalay Place)
(702) 632-7200

Celebrity chef (Rick Moonen) has lots of celebrity friends who tend to pop into his celebrity-friendly "steampunk" bistro as a prelude to a night of partying at MBay.

Sonny's Saloon
3449 Sammy Davis Jr Drive
(702) 731-5553

Sonny's claimed its place in infamy as the ransom-drop-off location in the 1993 kidnapping of Steve Wynn's daughter. Known back then as a hangout for off-shift casino employees, not much changed; the customers start pouring in around 11 p.m., with a mix of old-timers, dealers, dancers, and other working types who make for some amazing only-in-Vegas people watching.

STK Las Vegas (Cosmopolitan)
(702) 698-7990

From Tony Romo and Andre Agassi, to Halle Berry and Jessica Alba, via Robin Thicke and Dan Aykroyd, the steakhouse at Cosmo can certainly boast some star-studded carnivores among its clientele.

HALLE BERRY DINES AT STK LAS VEGAS

TAO Asian Bistro (Venetian/Grand Canal Shoppes)
(702) 388-8588

If gossip maven Perez Hilton chooses to dine here when he's in town, you know his likely won't be the only famous face in the house.

Additional Recommendations

SPECIAL DIET

DATE AND ARTICHOKE PIZZA FROM CRUSH

CRUSH (see page 209)

This celebrity hotspot at MGM Grand also caters to pretty much every "special-diet" need you can think of, with dedicated Vegan, Vegetarian, Gluten-Free, Dairy-Free, and Seafood/Shellfish-Free menus.

Divine Café at the Springs Preserve
333 S. Valley View Boulevard
(702) 822-7700

Casual health-conscious fare served within the setting of an urban-hiking and environmental-education treasure. Walk off your meal in the verdant Mojave diorama, then check out the excellent Nevada State Museum next door for some additional brain fodder.

EATT Healthy Food (see page 145)

A good selection of diet-friendly Gallic dishes, like mini quiches and ratatouille roulades. There's steak, but also lots of quinoa. A true find.

Go Raw Café (2 locations)

2381 E. Windmill Lane #18 / 2910 Lake East Drive (closed Sunday)
(702) 450-9007 / (702) 254-5382

A vegan raw bar and health food store operating since 2003, now with locations on both the east and west sides of town, serving a menu of live organic vegan cuisine and freshly made veggie juices.

Jacques Café

1910 Village Center Circle #1
(702) 550-6363

This neighborhood nook in Summerlin has a west coast-via-France vibe. Lots of quinoa and kale, but organic-raised beef in dishes, too.

Komol Restaurant

953 E. Sahara Avenue E-10
(702) 731-6542

If you don't want critters in your curry, hurry to this vegan-friendly Southeast Asian culinary gem (meat-eaters also welcome).

VEGGIE SALAD FROM KOMOL

Krayvings
11770 W. Charleston Boulevard #150
(702) 945-0520

Ignore the dumb spelling and enjoy the views while chomping on a surprisingly satisfying low-carb, low-fat, spinach-egg-white wrap ordered from a hi-tech tablet.

Lazeez Indian-Mediterranean Grill
8560 W. Desert Inn Road
(702) 778-1613

Indian-Middle Eastern halal eatery on the far west side of town, serving a menu that includes an array of vegan, vegetarian, and gluten-free options.

Mint Indian Bistro
730 E. Flamingo Road
(702) 894-9334

Las Vegas' top Indian restaurant caters to many special-diet needs, including offering separate vegan and vegetarian versions of the chef's tasting menu, not to mention halal meat, an array of gluten-free dishes and beers, and a selection of organic/vegan wines.

Osi's Kitchen
4604 W. Sahara Avenue #6
(702) 826-2727

VEGGIE VEGAN CURRY FROM MINT INDIAN BISTRO

A newcomer to Vegas' glatt Kosher dining scene, this affordable relative-owned Mediterranean-Moroccan café has been garnering rave reviews. Offers a range of catering menus for Shabbat Dinner.

Sprocket Bar and Restaurant
100 S. Green Valley Parkway, Henderson
(702) 361-8183

Whole Foods Market's new concept of in-store eateries is done outdoors in Green Valley. Vegan "black forbidden rice" sushi can be ordered next to pork-belly sliders, all with an impressive selection of beer on tap.

The Hummus Factory
7875 W. Sahara Avenue
(702) 675-6020

The rare food truck that made it to bricks (well, faux stucco anyway) in Las Vegas, it serves prodigious plates of salads, dips, shawarma, and more. Lots of sumac seasoning is used, a good sign.

VegeNation (see page 199)

Veggie House (see page 124)

Violette's
8560 W. Desert Inn Road
(702) 685-0466

Sin City vacationers are making the trek far from the Strip for artfully prepared tempeh-loaded dishes, other veggie-laden creations, and smoothies, of course. The Violette is Cyndi Violette, one of the original "poker babes" and a World Series of Poker bracelet winner (2004).

Wynn/Encore

Thanks to Steve Wynn's dalliance with veganism, every Wynn Resorts restaurant carries a "secret" veggie-friendly menu. You'll need to ask your server to see it (vegans note the odd dish may include dairy or honey, so check before you order). Also noteworthy, the Buffet at Wynn is renowned for its sugar-free dessert options.

DRINKING LAS VEGAS

WILBURN

Las Vegas is a living breathing thing. It's a sprawling organism in the barren desert, producing prosperity and all the good things about life in America. It's an animal of fun—and the blood running through its veins is alcohol.

For those of us who travel on their livers, half the pit stops we make when vacationing in a new city are entirely dedicated to putting together an expert bar crawl, and in this section, we hope to make that as easy as possible for you.

After all, among the three of us fine authors, we've had an ass on just about every bar stool in town. But I'm the guy you really need to talk to when it comes to drinks.

London has the pubs, Paris has the cafés, but Vegas has always had a solid hold on the best rough-and-tumble bars in the world.

The "dive bar" is where the story of Las Vegas gains its traction, the setting of a chance meeting that flings the protagonists of Vegas books and movies into whatever bizarre conflict they become embroiled in. To the theater of the mind, the characters on either side of the bar carry with them a soul native to Las Vegas and tales unique to our city. The drinks are scarcely any good, the food is almost inedible, but stepping into these dens of iniquity is an experience that can't be replicated. Whether you're flying into Vegas on Trump's 747 or hitching a ride in your cousin's '97 Saturn, no trip to Sin City is complete without a colorful night at one of these beer-stained hives.

But that's where any drinking distinction Las Vegas could ever claim started and ended. The evolution of mixology in Las Vegas, compared to the rest of the country, was at one time far behind the curve, laughable compared to many of the "cocktail cities" like San Francisco, New Orleans, or Seattle. There they were, breaking the boundaries of what makes a cocktail bar, while we were barely featuring anything more exciting than an espresso martini on a restaurant menu. Ah, but we had the great motivational force for any industry: lots and lots of Benjamins, baby. People saw dollar signs when guests were paying a premium for something new, interesting, and especially labor-intensive.

Within the span of only a couple years, money poured into the education, development, recruiting, and promotion of craft cocktails.

Hotshot bartenders made their mark by launching groundbreaking drink programs for new resorts, revamping the once-great restaurant bar (like Tony Abou-Ganim did at Bellagio), and even starting to put down tent posts off the Strip. Coinciding with the revitalization of downtown, plus some awards going to juggernauts such as Herbs & Rye, Las Vegas won its place in the national cocktail awareness fair and square.

Today in Las Vegas, multi-million-dollar purpose-built alcohol education centers exist like nowhere else (for example, the Spirit Academy at Southern Wine or the Alchemy Room at Wirtz Beverage, both liquor distributors), a restaurant can open without a signature cocktail list at the risk of being a laughingstock, and you can put as many miles on your liver as I have and still have a chance to be consistently surprised on every well-curated night out drinking. Yes, Las Vegas is a city for drinking; it always has been, it always will be.

BEER CULTURE

THILMONT

Bad Beat Brewing
7380 Eastgate Road #110, Henderson
(702) 463-4199

Try their basil-infused Ace in the Hole pale ale and play a few rounds of cornhole.

Banger Brewing
450 Fremont Street #135
(702) 456-2739

Tends toward malty brews. A decent place to chill on Fremont Street.

CraftHaus Brewery
7350 Eastgate Road #110, Henderson
(702) 415-9184

The arty and engaging tasting-room interior is filled with cuckoo clocks. Specializes in deliciously tart Belgian saisons. Look for the Dave Grohl pillow!

CRAFTHAUS BREWERY

Eating Las Vegas

Gordon Ramsay Pub & Grill (Caesars Palace)
(702) 731-7410

A slice of cool Britannia in hot Vegas. Quality food to match the beer selection.

Hofbräuhaus
4510 Paradise Road
(702) 853-2337

A Bavarian-sanctioned tourist magnet near the Hard Rock. Yes, there are giant steins to be drained.

Hop Nuts Brewing
1120 S. Main Street #150
(702) 816-5371

An independent brewery in downtown's Arts District. Fills up with funky folk.

Joseph James Brewing Company
155 Gibson Road, Henderson
(702) 454-2739

No tasting room, but look for these homegrown brews on taps around town.

Khoury's Fine Wine & Spirits
9915 S. Eastern Avenue
(702) 435-9463

Not only can you choose among hundreds and hundreds of pilsners, pale ales, porters, sours, stouts, and more from this booze bazaar's encyclopedic shelves, there's a small friendly bar with select seasonal beers on tap. They can pop the top on your retail purchases to enjoy in-house, too.

Lovelady Brewing
20 S. Water Street, Henderson
(702) 857-8469

One of the new breed of microbreweries in the metro area, Lovelady is housed in a cool Art Deco-revival building. Inside, it's all wood and metal in classic tasting-room form. The 9th Island Pineapple Sour wild ale is an excellent starter pour.

Money Plays
4755 W. Flamingo Road
(702) 368-1828

Among the absolute diviest places in this book. Ramshackle and smoke-filled. But the beer menu is extensive. Your call.

Pub 365 (Tuscany Suites and Casino)
(702) 893-8933

So unexpected for the location, Pub 365 has at least one beer to match every orbit of the sun around your parched personal planet. The cool handmade "Unicorn Books" are big wooden binders listing rare suds available, and most likely hard to find elsewhere in Vegas. An absolute gem.

Public House (Venetian/Grand Canal Shoppes)
(702) 407-5310

A fun and lively gastropub.

Public School 702
1850 Festival Plaza Drive
(702) 749-3007

Extremely popular outpost of a small southern California-based chain located in Downtown Summerlin. With a respectable rotation of brews, this place gets very busy.

Tenaya Creek Brewery
831 W. Bonanza Road
(702) 362-7335

Over the past year, Tenaya Creek Brewery has completely transformed its game for the better. The beers are now more varied and of a much higher quality. This is a fine facility with tanks and a pub—plus, there's a taxidermied jackalope on a wall!

Todd English P.U.B. (Shops at Crystals)
(702) 489-8080

Lots of beers on tap. Very dudely.

Triple 7 Restaurant and Microbrewery (Main Street Station)
(702) 387-1896

Check out the gigantic and lengthy antique bar imported from Florida while ordering a sampler.

COFFEE CULTURE

Café Leoné
400 S. Rampart Boulevard
(702) 684-5853

Looks like an Italian piazza, but with more plastic surgery on the clientele side. Notable for being thronged on weekends.

Coffee Hunter
7425 S. Eastern Avenue
(702) 586-5002

Henderson seems to be the current coffee hotspot of this radiant valley. And Coffee Hunter has the in-demand Stumptown brews, including cold varieties.

Makers & Finders Urban Coffee Bar (see page 158)

A very modern West Coasty place with a Latin inflection and rare beans.

Mothership Coffee Roasters
(see page 161)

It looks like a shop from Portland, Oregon, transplanted to a Henderson strip mall. Top-quality brews.

PublicUS (see page 198)

Hip quotient: off the register. But the espresso is worthy and comes

BEAN BAGS FROM MOTHERSHIP

out of a machine that looks like a UFO. Many mustaches and tattoos.

Sambalatte Torrefazione (multiple locations)
Monte Carlo
(702) 730-6789

This local chain is a real scene especially at Boca Park.

Select Starbucks (multiple locations)
Aria at CityCenter
starbucks.com

Yes, there are even a couple of cool spots to get a Clover cup, such as the modernistic glass-and-metal box east of the Strip by the Hughes Center, and the location in Aria.

Sunset Coffee House
3130 E. Sunset Road
(702) 433-3304

Where the art-loving coffee-fueled kiddos of Vegas (and Henderson) hang out.

DIVE BARS/
HIPSTER HANGOUTS

WILBURN

Aces and Ales (2 locations)
3740 S. Nellis Boulevard / 2801 N. Tenaya Way
(702) 436-7600 / (702) 638-2337

An institution of the Vegas "Beerluminatti," you'll find more rare and special brews here than almost anywhere else in town. Avoid the food, at least until you're well and thoroughly juiced.

Atomic Liquors
917 Fremont Street
(702) 982-3000

Big beards, girls with nose piercings, a communist-themed bicycle gang—you'll find them all here on any given night. Apparently, everyone loves a really good beer. For anyone who doesn't, the cocktails are really good, too.

Bunkhouse Saloon
124 S. 11th Street
(702) 982-1764

A place for young people to pretend they're slumming it, the live-music stage tends to grab some surprisingly good acts from genres that no one knows about (yet).

Champagne's
3557 S. Maryland Parkway
(702) 737-1699

As seen on "Bar Rescue," a bar that really didn't need rescuing. Good place to get a $2 "mystery shot."

Davy's Locker
1149 E. Desert Inn Road
(702) 735-0001

Pabst, pool, and pirate pictures.

Dealers Choice
4552 Spring Mountain Road
(702) 367-6798

Pool, pool, and more pool.

Eating Las Vegas

Dino's Lounge
1516 S. Las Vegas Boulevard
(702) 382-3894

Calling itself the "Last Neighborhood Bar" and lurking in the depths of "Naked City," Dino's is worth a visit if only for its people-watching potential (especially on Karaoke nights).

Dispensary Lounge
2451 E. Tropicana Avenue
(702) 458-6343

Part of the experience here is taking in the surroundings of the divey Dispensary, which proudly boasts of being open since 1976 without ever undergoing a renovation. The big water wheel and lawn furniture off the bar attest.

Double Down Saloon
4640 Paradise Road
(702) 791-5775

The floors are sticky with what I hope is beer, the signature cocktail is Ass Juice, and the bathroom isn't suitable for honest Christian bowel movements, but good God, no place personifies a dive bar better than the Double Down.

PONY RIDE AT DOUBLE DOWN SALOON

Four Kegs Sports Pub
276 N. Jones Boulevard
(702) 870-0255

Las Vegas' best Stromboli and beer so cold, ice forms in the mugs.

Frankie's Tiki Room
1712 W. Charleston Boulevard
(702) 385-3110

Drunks in the mornings and nerds at night, the atmosphere is always friendly. These drinks will knock you on your ass, but the rum selection and prices are what will really blow you away.

Hard Hat Lounge
1765 S. Industrial Road
(702) 384-8987

Prides itself on being "Las Vegas' Original and Diviest Dive Bar" since 1962 and an "unpretentious setting for getting loaded on a budget." Check the famous mural painted by Frank Bowers to settle a bar tab back in '63.

Huntridge Tavern
1116 E. Charleston Boulevard
(702) 384-7377

Very lived-in and accommodating to the ancient barflies, it's much less imposing than most of the rest. Enjoy the vintage Bud Dry promotional material and TCM on the tube.

Money Plays (see page 220)

Dreadlocked owner/bartender "Big Stan" describes his lively joint just west of the Palms that features a first-rate shuffleboard table and world-class jukebox as "the best place to slum in Vegas." No argument here.

Moon Doggies Bar & Grill
3240 Arville Street #F
(702) 368-4180

SCOOTERS OUTSIDE MONEY PLAYS

Get Buffalo-style pizza, wings, and sandwiches from the Naked City Pizza Shop located inside.

Eating Las Vegas

Oddfellows
150 Las Vegas Boulevard Suite 190
(702) 336-3235

An amazing place for people watching, though looking normal will make you the oddball in this crowd. The '80s dance-party nights pour on the nostalgia of an era in which most of this joint's regular crowd hadn't even been conceived.

PublicUS (see page 198)

Hallowed purveyor of the most rarified toasted-bean juice created by perfectionists for connoisseurs and their acolytes. The food's decent too, if somewhat overpriced.

Sand Dollar Lounge
3355 Spring Mountain Road
(702) 485-5401

Where industry folks go for a no-frills night out, the drinks here are solid and come accompanied by dadrock bands and shuffleboard.

Additional Recommendations

Shifty's
3805 W. Sahara Avenue
(702) 871-4952

While it's not obvious that you can even get food here, this place serves one of the least expensive steak deals in town—$6-$12.

Stage Door
4000 Linq Lane
(702) 733-0124

This slots-only bar is within walking distance of the Strip. It sells bottled beer for a buck and shots for three. Get a quarter-pound hot dog and a beer for $3 around the clock.

Velveteen Rabbit
1218 S. Main Street
(702) 685-9645

The house music and funky aesthetic attracts the crowds, the light show and painstakingly hand-crafted cocktails keep them here.

VELVETEEN RABBIT BAR

MIXOLOGY CULTURE

ATOMIC LIQUORS FULL BAR

Atomic Liquors (see page 223)

Jewel of the downtown drinking lineup, Atomic has a stunning selection of both interesting cocktails and craft beers. No downtown visit is complete without a trip to the city's oldest watering hole.

Carnevino (Essential 50: see page 14)

Few gastronomic experiences surpass an aged steak and an intriguing cocktail enjoyed in one of the last bastions of the gentleman bartender, where an expertise in etiquette is matched by intoxicating improvisation skills.

Delmonico Steakhouse (Essential 50: see page 50)

An encyclopedic whisky selection forms the backdrop for cocktail trend-setting head bartender Juyong Kang, whose potions are mixed with magical intuition.

DELMONICO STEAKHOUSE BAR

Additional Recommendations

229

Downtown Cocktail Room
111 S. Las Vegas Boulevard
(702) 880-3696

The drinks here are high-concept and painstakingly curated. This can be a very relaxing spot … before the DJ arrives.

Golden Tiki
3939 Spring Mountain Road
(702) 222-3196

As if Trader Vic and Walt Disney built a bar together, it truly doesn't get more "tiki" than this. The cocktails are impeccable and the décor is a cornucopia of kitsch.

Herbs & Rye (see page 203)

The ace in Vegas' mixology deck, H&R is home to a cocktail dream team led by Nectaly Mendoza, named "Bartender of the Year" in the 2016 Nightclub & Bar Awards.

HERBS & RYE BAR

Libertine Social (Mandalay Bay)
(877) 632-7700

The drink program here is already out of this world, created by mixology legend Tony Abou-Ganim. Be sure to check out the Arcade Bar, located toward the back of the restaurant. The special menu there is geared toward the even more adventurous drinker.

Velveteen Rabbit
(see page 228)

Anything where the menu is printed as part of an art zine is sure to be hip, and this is the closest we have to an ultra-hip San Francisco mixology bar. Here you can find some of the most inventive mind-bending cocktails in Vegas.

BASIC BITCH DRINK AT VELVETEEN RABBIT

FERRARO'S

GRAPE EXPECTATIONS
(LAS VEGAS' BEST WINE DRINKING)

Las Vegas isn't really a "wine bar" sort of town. Wine bars generally require a certain level of introspection and contemplation and Las Vegas generally is about as contemplative as a UFC cage match. But this doesn't mean there aren't fabulous places to indulge your taste for fermented grapes. What it does mean is that you have to go to some of our finer restaurants to find wines (by the glass or bottle) that will blow your socks off.

Below are my 12 favorite sipping venues, places where our town's great sommeliers take enormous pride in pouring vintages from around the globe—wines you can drink, or think about, to your palate's content.

Estiatorio Milos

Greek wines may be unpronounceable, but they're delicious. They're also substantially underpriced compared to similar seafood-friendly wines from France and Italy. Don't even try to master the odd lisps and tongue rolls of Assyrtiko, Moshofilero, or Mavrodaphne.

Just point and smile, or ask the staff for help. (I promise they won't make fun of you.) Anyone who orders anything but Greek wines with this food should be sentenced to a year of drinking nothing but Harvey Wallbangers.

Restaurant Guy Savoy

The list is as thick as a dictionary and, at first blush, not for the faint of heart or parsimonious of purse. But look closely and you'll find a surprising number of bargains for less than $100. Or ask sommelier Phil Park and he'll happily point them out to you. The champagne bar is where you'll find serious oenophiles perusing the list a full half-hour before their reservation, just like they do it in France.

Chada Street/Chada Thai & Wine

These sister restaurants are a few miles apart, but connected by

Additional Recommendations

233

a love of white wines that owner Bank Atcharawan has successfully brought to Chinatown. Both lists are deep in Rieslings and chardonnays; the champagne selection at Chada Street puts most Strip lists to shame and at decidedly gentler prices. It's not for nothing that every sommelier in Las Vegas treats both of these venues like their personal after-hours clubs.

Marché Bacchus

A pinot noir wall, lakeside dining, and the gentlest mark-ups in town ($10 over retail) make MB a must-stop on any wine-lover's tour of Vegas. Jeff and Rhonda Wyatt are always there to help you choose a glass or a case of whatever mainstream cab or off-beat syrah suits your fancy. Or do what I do: Just stick with Burgundy and go nuts.

Ferraro's Italian Restaurant & Wine Bar

What I love about Italian wines is what I love about Italians and Italian food: They're friendly, passionate, fiercely regional, and confusing in a good way. Don't know your Montelcinos from your Montepulcianos? Nessun problema. Geno Ferraro is always there to help you parse the Barbarescos from the Barolos. One of the greatest Italian lists in America is at one of our finest Italian restaurants.

Bazaar Meat

I don't understand Spanish wine any more than I understand how José Andrés can have so much energy and so many great restaurants. But the next best thing to knowing a lot about a country's wines is knowing a sommelier who is eager to teach you. In Las Vegas, Chloe Helfand is that gal. She's always there with a smile and a lip-smacking wine you don't know made with a grape you've never heard of. Which is one of the reasons we love sommeliers. And Chloe.

La CAVE

Mark Hefter's wine program is a lot like Mark Hefter: fun, interesting, intelligent, and all over the map. Hefter has poured wine from Le Cirque 2000 in New York to Spago and Circo in Las Vegas and needless to say, the man knows his grapes. With over 50 wines by the glass, he can dazzle anyone, from the novice drinker to the dedicated oenophile. But what we love about his list is its eclecticism.

Eating Las Vegas

At La Cave, you can dip your toe into the world's most interesting wines at very friendly price points. Curious about those orange and pink wines that are all the rage these days? Here's where to start.

Carnevino

If your measure of a great wine bar is the number of wines by the glass offered, look elsewhere. If you rate your wine tasting by quality—of the breadth and depth of the list, the bar snacks, the staff, and the mixology (should you stray into creative boozy territory)—then this is your place. The list is conveniently located inside the (massive) menu and the mark-ups are not for the timid. But the excellence of everything, from the steaks and pastas to the super Tuscan verticals, will take your breath away.

Lotus of Siam

Robert Parker (yeah, that Robert Parker) calls Lotus' wine card the greatest for German wines in America and we have no reason to argue with him. It's also shoulder-deep in sake, Alsatian whites, and Austrian Grüner Veltliners—all of which match (in surprising ways) Saipan Chutima's fierce and fiery country-Thai cooking. This is where you'll find almost every wine professional in town on their day off, usually at a table groaning with bottles of Riesling.

Sage

The trouble with Sage is that the food is so good, sometimes you forget about the wine, and the wine list is so good, sometimes you forget about the food. I like California pinot noir and chardonnay with Shawn McClain's innovative fare, but the list covers the world in all areas of consequence. Such choices here are a happy conundrum to experience, whether you're dining or hanging out in the stunning bar.

Hearthstone

Great wine drinking in the 'burbs is harder to find than a corner without a fast-food franchise. Hearthstone deserves props for actually having a wine program and for a list that breaks down according to varietal character—"Big Reds," "Crisp, Clean & Lean," "Voluptuous But Light," etc. The by-the-glass selection is solid, but what really gets my attention is the half-off Monday-night specials, which al-

Additional Recommendations

235

low for some serious drinking of some serious bottles. That discount only counts for bottles under a Benjamin, but if you've got 20 to 30 of them, $2,500 for a bottle of '05 DRC Echezeaux, or $2,800 for some Screaming Eagle, are flat-out steals.

Bin 702

Downtown Las Vegas is so wine-challenged, it makes Summerlin look like Napa Valley. Amidst all the bars and hipster hangouts, though, this teeny tiny space in Container Park holds forth with a small selection of interesting reds and whites from around the globe, most in the $30-$60 range. Wine snobs will be underwhelmed, but for those looking for a break from craft cocktails and exotic coffees, it's an oasis.

SANGRIA BLANCO AT HEARTHSTONE

Section IV

Index and Maps

Essential 50 Restaurants Index
(Casino Locations)

Essential 50 Restaurants Index
(Non-Casino Locations by nearest major cross streets)

All Restaurants Index

All Restaurants Index

All Restaurants Index

All Restaurants Index

All Restaurants Index

JOHN CURTAS has been covering the Las Vegas food and restaurant scene since 1995. His "Food For Thought" commentaries ran for 15 years on KNPR Nevada Public Radio, and these days he can be seen every Friday as Las Vegas' "Favorite Foodie" on KSNV's (NBC) Channel 3's "Wake Up With the Wagners." He has written reviews for more magazines and guidebooks than he can count and has appeared multiple times as a judge on "Iron Chef America" and "Top Chef Masters." In addition, he also authors the Eating Las Vegas food blog (www.eatinglv.com). This fifth edition of this book reflects his 31 years of eating in more restaurants, more often, than anyone in the history of Las Vegas.

GREG THILMONT is a food and travel writer who has been on the Vegas cuisine scene since 2005. His work has been featured in publications including Lonely Planet, MSN Travel, *Desert Companion*, *Las Vegas Magazine*, *Las Vegas Weekly*, and Vegas.com. The first piece of writing Greg was ever paid for was for a story on the history of bagels in his college newspaper. He has bachelor's and master's degrees in English Literature from the University of Utah. This is his second edition as a co-author of *Eating Las Vegas*.

MITCHELL WILBURN is a native of Las Vegas, an obsessive gourmand, and a passionate expert on all things fermented, distilled, or fortified. He has held positions as restaurant critic for *Las Vegas CityLife*, the Condé Nast Travel Network, and NPR's *Desert Companion Magazine*, and has contributed to a myriad of trade publications, cocktail blogs, food-news sites, tourism magazines, and John Curtas' own EatingLV.com. He even had an anonymous, unsanctioned, self-published counterculture futurist/transhumanist philosophy zine back in his days at the University of Nevada Las Vegas, and no, you may not see it.

ZUCCOTTA AT ANDRES